A Practical Guide to Alternative Dispute Resolution in Personal Injury Claims: Getting the Most Out of ADR Post-Jackson

Peter Causton MA (Cantab),

Solicitor Advocate and Barrister at Law,

Deputy District Judge, International Online Mediator,

Civil and Commercial Mediator (ProMediate (UK) Limited)

Nichola Evans (LLB & MCIARB),

Partner Browne Jacobson LLP,

Board Member of Civil Mediation Council,

Law Society Council Member – Forum of Insurance Lawyers,

Law Society Civil Justice Committee

James Arrowsmith MA(Oxon) Juris,

Partner Browne Jacobson LLP,

Forum of Insurance Lawyers ADR Special Focus Team member

Law Brief Publishi

D1610025

Published 2016 by
Law Brief Publishing
30 The Parks
Minehead
Somerset
TA24 8BT

www.lawbriefpublishing.com

Paperback: 978-1-911035-09-1

PREFACE

Litigation is increasingly viewed as a last resort and alternative means of resolving disputes is encouraged. Personal injury claims are no exception.

Briggs LJ, the architect of the Online Solutions Court commented that the creation of the court will bring alternative dispute resolution into the mainstream and it will make resolution by the parties the cultural norm, rather than something alternative to the mainstream. In short, he says, it seeks to take the "A" out of "ADR". "If this new Court takes off and the public gets to like resolving their civil disputes in this less adversarial solutions based way, who knows to what level of claim it may eventually be extended upwards" he said.

The purpose of this book is to explain the options available to litigants, how it may develop in the future, and to set out the various ADR options available, so that the reader is ready for the revolution.

Personal injury practitioners frequently use ADR to resolve personal injury claims, whether by joint settlement meetings, negotiating between solicitors or by using the Portal. What they do not use so much is mediation or arbitration. With the changing claims environment and the resulting pressures to find better ways to resolve disputes practitioners who wish to remain competitive must re-examine their practices, to explore the benefits of other approaches to dispute resolution and ways to improve existing practices. If, as we suspect, personal injury claims are included in the "Online Solutions Court" and the small claims limit is increased, conciliation or mediation will form a key part of the process, and those already using these dispute resolution procedure will be well prepared to take advantage of this.

Nonetheless, there is resistance to this change. One practitioner told us "We mediate rarely in clinical negligence. I'm a big fan of a Joint Settlement Meeting. The mediation took over 14 hours – mainly due to the mediator I think. It will take me a long time to recommend that course of settlement to my clients again! It may have been an anomaly, but it was definitely a painful experience."

However, mediation has been shown to have a high success rate and the NHS Litigation Authority has recently announced plans to establish their mediation panel. It is clear that a progressive approach to ADR can pay dividends, notwithstanding the occasional negative anecdote. Mediation need not take 14 hours or be an expensive process, as there are various options available. It is not a case of "one size fits all". There are telephone mediations and time limited and online options available. Just as the Courts are changing to introduce new technology, mediation and ADR are also changing to become more flexible.

While personal injury practitioners tend to strongly favour JSMs and negotiation when it comes to ADR, we see different trends in other sectors, with mediation and arbitration much more 'the norm' in some commercial sectors, for example. There are opportunities for personal injury practitioners to broaden their dispute resolution horizons to assist them in finding the best means of resolving their client's case. Understanding the range of options will help practitioners choose the best form of ADR and reduce painful experiences such as that described above.

We predict that ADR will to be used more in personal injury claims, and will eventually become a genuine alternative to Court proceedings, rather than something to be fitted in to case management directions just before trial. Automated processes will be introduced and costs will not be recoverable, meaning that there will be pressure to resolve claims early on,

This book aims to explore those options and to provide practical guidance to assist practitioners to using ADR to maximum effect in their cases today, and to prepare their practices for increased emphasis on ADR as the preferred means of dispute resolution in the future.

Peter Causton
Nichola Evans
James Arrowsmith
October 2016

Contents

CHAPTER ONE
WHAT IS ADR?

ADR means Alternative Dispute Resolution. This is a term with a very wide definition and covers any form of dispute resolution, other than through Court process. Strictly speaking the term "alternative" may be something of a misnomer. Most forms of ADR are used hand in glove with either litigation or arbitration.

ADR comes in a range of forms, as summarized below. Most of these forms of ADR are discussed in further detail later on in the book.

Early neutral evaluation

"Early neutral evaluation" can be organised at any stage in proceedings. The procedure involves a Judge, an arbitrator or an independent third party (for example a solicitor, or a barrister) sitting with the parties and, on the basis of written evidence put before them (for example documents and witness statements) and on the basis of what they hear from the parties, giving a non-binding view as to the likely outcome of a legal dispute. If the parties have used a Judge in litigation for early neutral evaluation, then if the case does not settle that Judge will not try the case. They will have no further involvement in the procedural aspects of the case.

The courts can also order ENE pursuant to their powers under CPR3. This has not been much used in personal injury claims, though some court centres do use it. However, Briggs LJ is a proponent of ENE and if his Review is implemented, it will feature in the new Online Solutions Court system.

Arbitration

Arbitration falls within the broad umbrella of ADR, but arbitration also has much in common with litigation. Comparing litigation and arbitration the similarities are obvious: there are two (and perhaps more) adversaries, there is generally a formal process for the exchange of pleadings, disclosure of documents, service of witness reports and expert reports, albeit that it is a process that the parties control and dictate the terms. If necessary, parties can be compelled to comply with deadlines.

In each case the process culminates with one or more hearings. At the conclusion of the hearing or hearings there will be some form of determination on the issues which remain live between the parties. Generally there will be a winner and a loser. A number of consequences will flow from that determination, notably in terms of who bears the costs or a large part of the costs of the whole process. Arbitration is currently being promoted as a way of resolving personal injury claims without going to Court, but the costs of the arbitration being suggested are still relatively high compared to other methods of ADR. This is due to the involvement of an arbitrator throughout the process and that they tend to be relatively senior. Given the increases in Court fees and with the expectation that they will increase further, the balance is shifting, however, and some personal injury lawyers are increasingly turning to arbitration as a way of dealing with matters in a more cost effective manner.

Joint Settlement Meetings

A JSM is essentially a forum within which negotiation will take place. On the run up to a JSM, parties will have exchanged evidence and details of their case. At the JSM itself the parties and their representatives will have the opportunity to set out their case to one another (typically through their representatives) and exchange offers. There is no facilitator or decision maker in a JSM and so if the parties cannot compromise with one another, there will be no resolution to the dispute.

Mediation

Mediation may be facilitative or evaluative.

Facilitative mediation has some similarities with a JSM, but with the addition of a mediator who will assist the parties in exploring their own cases, identifying their objectives and moving towards a settlement, by acting as a neutral, independent, trusted diplomat assisting the parties to resolve their differences.

Evaluative mediation has features in common with early neutral evaluation. While the mediator will remain a neutral party, they will be prepared to express views on the issues and arguments which arise at the mediation, generally with all parties present. They may go so far as to express a view on an appropriate settlement. Having contributed their views to the process, in order to encourage the parties to scrutinize their case and their opponents, the mediator will then endeavor to broker a deal.

Pre Action protocols

These are processes in which parties are expected to engage prior to litigation, which create opportunities for settlement, typically through exchange of offers (although they require parties to consider other forms of ADR and there is no reason why other ADR should not take place).

In this book we will consider the protocols for low value injury relating to motor, employers Liability and public liability claims. These are supplemented by a "Stage 3" process to bring a dispute on quantum of a claim before a judge for a decision with a minimum of cost.

Other pre action protocols are in place for personal injury claims not falling within the low value process and for clinical negligence claims.

Part 36

Though not commonly thought of as ADR, Part 36 is a key feature in any practitioner's dispute resolution armory, and is designed to encourage settlement through a system of incentives and penalties with a view to cutting through cases and resolving matters at an early stage.

Summary

- There are various forms of ADR including

  o Early neutral evaluation

  o Arbitration

  o Joint Settlement Meetings

  o Mediation

- We have also included the Pre-Action Protocols and the Part 36 offer processes in this book because they are an important part of trying to resolve cases at an early stage used by personal injury practitioners.

CHAPTER TWO
HOW THE COURTS
ENCOURAGE ADR

Jackson LJ who masterminded the reforms to civil litigation in 2013, was primarily concerned with reducing the costs of litigation. He identified that one of the ways of doing this was by using ADR and particularly mediation. He commented in his report that *"ADR (particularly mediation) has a vital role to play in reducing the costs of civil disputes, by fomenting the early settlement of cases."* ADR is, in his view under-used. He believed that its potential benefits are not as well known as they should be. He stated that there *"should be a serious campaign (a) to ensure that all litigation lawyers and judges are properly informed about the benefits which ADR can bring, and (b) to alert the public and small businesses to the benefits of ADR."* He recommended the publication of an ADR Handbook, the first edition of which was published in 2013 and distributed to every civil judge. The second edition has recently been published.

Court Rules supporting ADR

Implementation of the Jackson reforms is creating an environment whereby ADR is becoming more attractive and parties are encouraged to settle difficult disputes earlier.

One result of the reforms is that parties have to comply more rigidly with the rules and also have to predict then manage litigation budgets. Sanctions are more likely to be applied to defaulting parties. Court fees have also increased, so that parties pay enhanced fees that is more than their case will cost the Court Service to run. This amounts to 5% of the claim, up to a cap of £10,000, which is a significant sum. Non-recoverability of success fees for claimants and qualified one way costs shifting mean even successful parties in a typical injury claim will expect to incur some financial cost.

Jackson is also proposing fixed costs throughout the litigation system for cases up to £250,000 which is likely to concentrate lawyers' minds and encourage them to resolve claims before costs exceed recoverable costs.

For all of these reasons, litigation is becoming increasingly unattractive, and increasingly something to be embarked upon only once a case is close to being crystallised. There is therefore a greater incentive for parties reaching the point at which they are ready to litigate to consider their alternatives. A case that is appropriately prepared for court proceedings could well be sufficiently developed for mediation or some other form of ADR.

The rules add additional processes and incentives to engage in pre-action ADR. The 'Practice Direction - Pre-Action Conduct' identifies one of its aims as being to "enable parties to settle the issue between them without the need to start proceedings" and states that this is to be achieved "by encouraging the parties to consider using a form of Alternative Dispute Resolution ("ADR")" : see PD paragraphs 1 and 8 - particularly the latter. Consequently, the failure to consider, or to propose, or respond to proposals, for pre-action ADR may become relevant when considering orders in case-management, as well as to costs orders. The pre-action protocols also contain express provision for ADR; see particularly:- a) Pre-Action Protocol for Personal Injury Claims: paragraphs 2.16 – 2.19, b) Pre-Action Protocol for the Resolution of Clinical Disputes: paragraph 5, c) Pre-Action Protocol for Disease and Illness Claims: paragraph 2A.

Judicial support for ADR

It is clear from recent decisions that the courts wish to press home the message that litigation is intended to be a last resort and the system would be a success if like the "nuclear deterrent" it was seldom used. It is clear that parties should no longer engage in "no holds barred" litigation (Barbara Joyce Lilleyman v (1) Nigel Paul Lilleyman and others [2012] EWHC 1056 (Ch)) without considering proportionality, which is now part of the overriding objective. Parties are encouraged to use ADR early. To quote Sir Rupert Jackson:

> *"Of course there are many cases where a strict determination of rights and liabilities is what the parties require. The Courts stand ready to deliver such a service to litigants and must do so as expeditiously and economically as practicable. But before embarking upon full blooded adversarial litigation parties should first explore the possibility of settlement." (Faidi v Elliot Corporation [2012] EWCA Civ 287) - "As it is, neither side wrote to the other proposing mediation until shortly before the hearing in the Court of Appeal. By then huge costs had been incurred. …The total costs thrown away amount to £140,134. If the parties were driven by concern for the well being of lawyers, they could have given half that sum to the Solicitors Benevolent Association and then resolved their dispute for a modest fraction of the monies left over."*

While these cases provide examples of judicial encouragement of ADR, to Briggs LJ in his review of the Modernisation of the Chancery Division carried out in 2013, the judiciary is still not doing enough. This is also reflected in his Review of the Structure of the Civil Courts, completed in July 2016.

Briggs LJ favours a more structured approach, rather than leaving the extent of encouragement given by the judiciary to individual discretion, with no national policy, guidance or training being provided. He says the general approach is to treat alternative dispute resolution (ADR) as a completely separate process and that, save for the occasional word of encouragement, the making of space in a timetable for a stay, and the "very occasional" imposition of costs sanctions for unreasonable refusal, the approach is to let the parties get on with it. While recognising the advantages in having unwavering case management towards trial, he does think the court should take a more active role in the encouragement, facilitation and management of dispute resolution in the widest sense. He would like to see a change of culture amongst litigators.

We will look in more detail at the courts' ability to require ADR and sanctions for failure to engage in a later chapter.

Summary

The Courts are encouraging ADR by:

- Supporting the use of ADR in case management by ordering stays.

- Penalising parties who refuse to follow the pre-action protocols or to take part in ADR in costs.

CHAPTER THREE
THE DEVELOPMENT OF ADR AS
PART OF THE COURT SYSTEM

It has long been recognised that litigation is costly and time-consuming and that the majority of cases issued in the Courts settle before trial, so ADR has grown in popularity over the years. People have long predicted that the use of ADR will take off, but to date the annual CEDR mediation survey has not seen any dramatic increase and the prediction has not been reflected in reality. That may now be set to change as society moves away from formal Court procedures to resolving disputes on a private basis.

Meanwhile the Courts are trying to keep up, modernise, and encourage ADR. As set out in previous chapters, the litigation process is becoming increasingly unattractive to litigants, with high costs (part of which will inevitably be irrecoverable) and risks to both parties.

The front-loading of cases in the Civil Court system has carried on apace with the re-vamping of the pre-action protocols. These provide that sanctions for non-compliance may include adverse costs orders and the exclusion of an award of interest.

To add to this deterrent we see recent Court decisions imposing sanctions on parties for failing to engage in mediation, whereby silence in the face of an invitation to mediate is itself unreasonable conduct. These support the view that everyone has to engage in ADR first, or face the consequences down the line. However, as Briggs LJ has observed, application of these rules is inconsistent.

In the Small Claims Track, the Court's small claims mediation service also operates where the parties agree to mediate (save in respect of personal injury claims). With increasing numbers of litigants in person, and the challenges this creates in relation to court resource, judges recognise mediation as a valuable alternative to judicial determination of a claim in these cases. However, anecdotal evidence suggests that parties are agreeing to use the existing Small Claims Mediation service in order to delay proceedings, with cases being stayed for six weeks for mediation and then returning to the system afterwards for directions, not having been settled.

The Chancery Modernisation report of Briggs LJ suggested introducing the idea of FDRs (Family Dispute Resolution hearings) and early neutral evaluation into the Court process, so that judges can actively encourage settlement at an early stage. These recommendations have since been broadened and ensconced within a vision for online dispute resolution.

The Civil Justice Council's ("CJC") Online Dispute Resolution Advisory Group's report on Online Dispute Resolution for Low Value Claims (under £25,000) was published in 2015, recommended the creation of a virtual Court system, to be known as the HM Online Courts. The CJC Report proposed radical changes to the system, to involve ADR and to reduce the number of cases being taken to trial. There would be a filter to resolve disputes prior to reaching the final adjudicatory stage. This would involve a three tier system with Tier Two involving Online Facilitation. It is proposed that in order to bring a dispute to a speedy, fair conclusion without the involvement of judges, this service will provide online facilitators. Communicating via the Internet, these individuals will review papers and statements and help parties through mediation and negotiation. They will be supported where necessary, by telephone conferencing facilities. Additionally, there will be some automated negotiation, which are systems that help parties resolve their differences without the intervention of human experts.

The new system would be designed to minimise the need for lawyers. The idea is that early neutral evaluation on the papers should be the default position, telephone or internet hearings should be held as necessary and hearings on Court or Tribunal premises should only be held in rare cases. Parties would be given the option of accepting the Court Officer's assessment or to take the matter further and that if no objection is raised to the assessment, then the decision would become final and binding.

The recommendations were adopted in Briggs LJ's review of the Structure of the Civil Courts, which proposed the creation of an Online Solutions Court, which would involve ADR at the second stage as well as signposting to ADR at the first stage. The proposals also included reactivating the National Mediation Helpline and the after hours Court based mediation scheme. Briggs LJ also praised the small claims resolution hearings that take place in some Courts and result in settlement of small claims without a full hearing. If implemented, this would result in more use of ADR within the Court system and referral of cases to the external out of hours service for higher value cases.

So far as personal injury claims in the online solutions court is concerned, Briggs' recommendation is to exclude fast and multi track claims, and to permit voluntary inclusion of small claims, which may amount to a significant volume if the small claims limit is increased. However, as will be seen, other IT based systems are in place for some injury claims, and it is quite conceivable that in the future the online solutions court scheme will be extended. In any event, we envisage an indirect effect on injury claims as increased emphasis on ADR carries over into the broader court system, and as practitioners look for alternatives to the online solutions court to deliver efficient, effective dispute resolution for their clients.

Summary

- ADR is becoming an integral part of the Court system thanks to the Small Claims mediation service and the proposed online Court system.

- There is likely to be further integration with the Court system with the reestablishment of the National Mediation Helpline envisaged by Briggs LJ.

CHAPTER FOUR
THE PRE-ACTION PROTOCOLS

6 April 2015 saw the introduction of new protocols for personal injury and clinical negligence claims dovetailing with increases in Court fees. The terms of the updated protocols are important for practitioners, whether acting for claimants or defendants, as there are some important changes and the protocols now have added "teeth".

The Pre-Action Protocols, which need to be followed before starting Court proceedings, have been amended to actively encourage ADR. The new Pre-Action Protocol Practice Direction, setting out the best practice that the Courts expert parties to follow pre-proceedings makes it clear that parties must consider ADR, respond to offers and those failing to do so should expect to face sanctions.

It identifies one of its aims as being to enable parties to settle issues without recourse to the Courts, including the use of ADR, and the failure to consider, or to propose, or respond to proposals, for pre-action ADR may become relevant when considering orders in case-management, as well as to costs orders. It explains that Court proceedings should be a last resort. The parties should consider whether some form of alternative dispute resolution procedure might enable them to settle their dispute without commencing court proceedings, and if so, endeavour to agree which form to adopt. The Protocol explains that parties may negotiate to settle a dispute or may use a form of ADR including:

1. mediation – a third party facilitating a resolution;

2. arbitration – a third party deciding the dispute;

3. early neutral evaluation – a third party giving an informed opinion on the dispute;

4. adjudication – a process by which an independent adjudicator provides the parties with a decision that can resolve the dispute either permanently or on a temporary basis, pending subsequent court determination; and

5.   Ombudsmen schemes.

The Pre-Action Protocol Practice Direction makes it clear that:

> *"If proceedings are issued, the parties may be required by the court to provide evidence that ADR has been considered. A party's silence in response to an invitation to participate or a refusal to participate in ADR might be considered unreasonable by the court and could lead to the court ordering that party to pay additional court costs."* and *"The court may decide that there has been a failure of compliance when a party has "unreasonably refused to use a form of ADR, or failed to respond at all to an invitation to do so."*

So, the goal posts have moved in that parties are now very much expected to have tried ADR before starting proceedings, rather than during them.

Paragraph 4.6 of the Practice Direction specifically identifies sanctions the court may impose which include:

> *(1) "staying (that is suspending) the proceedings until steps which ought to have been taken have been taken;*

> *(2) an order that the party at fault pays the costs, or part of the costs, of the other party or parties (this may include an order under rule 27.14 (2) (g) in cases allocated to the small claims track);*

> *(3) an order that the party at fault pays those costs on an indemnity basis (rule 44.3 (3) sets out the definition of the assessment of costs on an indemnity basis);*

> *(4) if the party at fault is the claimant in whose favour an order for the payment of a sum of money is subsequently made, an order that the claimant is deprived of interest on all or part of that sum, and/or that interest is awarded at a lower rate than would otherwise have been awarded;*

> *(5) if the party at fault is a defendant, and an order for the payment of a sum of money is subsequently made in favour of the*

claimant, an order that the defendant pay interest on all or part of that sum at a higher rate, not exceeding 10% above base rate, than would otherwise have been awarded."

The message running throughout the new protocol is that proceedings should be the last resort. Nearly every Pre-Action Protocol now says:

"The parties should consider whether some form of alternative dispute resolution procedure would be more suitable than litigation, and if so, endeavour to agree which form to adopt. Both the Claimant and professional may be required by the Court to provide evidence that alternative means of resolving their dispute were considered. The Courts take the view that litigation should be a last resort"

The penalties which can now be imposed on parties failing to engage with the new protocol are as follows:

- Those who default can be ordered to pay the costs of the proceedings, or a significant proportion of them on the indemnity basis.

- If a claimant is at fault and is awarded monetary damages, the claimant's entitlement to interest can be withdrawn or interest awarded at a lower rate and for a lesser period. If the defendant is the offending party then they can be ordered to pay interest on the damages awarded to the claimant at a higher rate, capped at 10% above base rate.

If proceedings are started the claimant, to comply with para.9.7, should state in the claim form or particulars of claim whether the Practice Direction, and protocol, have been complied with.

The message is clear, if you don't take part in ADR, you risk sanctions. With respect to the revised Personal Injury Protocol, it even states that if a party to the claim does not have a legal representative, and so is a litigant in person, they should still, in so far as reasonably possible, fully comply with the Protocol.

Failure to Comply with the Pre-Action Protocols

There are authorities for the proposition that failure to comply with the Pre-Action Protocol can lead to costs consequences, similarly to failure to undertake ADR and/or mediation. Compliance with the Protocol is one of the factors that the Court takes into account when it comes to consider the issue of costs, as it is relevant to the issue of conduct.

The most recent decision on this is that of Jane Laporte v The Commissioner of Police of the Metropolis. In this case, the claimants lost, but sought to argue that there should be no order for costs because the defendant refused to engage in ADR.

The general rules about costs are to be found in CPR Part 44. CPR 44.2(1) provides that decisions relating to costs are in the discretion of the court:

> *(1) The court has discretion as to –*
>
> *(a) whether costs are payable by one party to another;*
>
> *(b) the amount of those costs; and*
>
> *(c) when they are to be paid.*

CPR 44.2(2) establishes the general rule that costs will follow the event:

> *(2) If the court decides to make an order about costs –*
>
> *(a) the general rule is that the unsuccessful party will be ordered to pay the costs of the successful party; but*
>
> *(b) the court may make a different order.*

CPR 44.2(4) identifies the circumstances to which the court is to have regard when exercising its discretion in making decisions about costs:

> *(4) In deciding what order (if any) to make about costs, the court will have regard to all the circumstances, including –*

(a) the conduct of all the parties;

(b) whether a party has succeeded on part of its case, even if that party has not been wholly successful; and

(c) any admissible offer to settle made by a party which is drawn to the court's attention, and which is not an offer to which costs consequences under Part 36 apply.

The term "alternative dispute resolution" ("ADR") is defined in the glossary to the CPR as a "collective description of methods of resolving disputes otherwise than through the normal trial process". One such process is mediation, but ADR forms part of the pre-action protocols.

The claimants pointed out that the defendants never provided a practice direction response to the letter of claim, in spite of its express agreement to do so and two chasing letters from the claimants' representatives. When no response was received by the agreed second extended deadline, the claimants sought a response by a further date. No response was received on this date or on any date thereafter.

Having considered each of the factors listed in Halsey and having regard to other circumstances and arguments raised in addition, the Court have formed the view that the defendant failed, without adequate (or adequately articulated) justification to engage in ADR which had a reasonable prospect of success. In addition, the Court needed to look at the matter in the round as a result of which it had to consider the separate issues arising from the criticisms raised of the defendant's failure to respond to the letter before action. The Court found that:

"the defendant undoubtedly ought to have responded to the letter before action more timeously and it is unsurprising that the claimants eventually lost patience and proceeded to plead their case formally. Had this been the only valid criticism of the procedural failings of the defendant I may well have concluded that it did not justify any substantive costs consequences. However, I have reached the view that the failure to respond in time was to prove to have been symptomatic of a sustained inability to prioritise the progress of this case thereafter and, in particular, to allocate sufficient time,

attention and/or resources to dealing with ADR in parallel to sub-
stantive preparation. This lends further corroboration to my view
that the defendant stumbled past ADR on the way to the hearing
rather than engaging with it with proportionate commitment and
focus. To this limited extent only, therefore, do I take the non-com-
pliance with the pre-action protocol into account."

Failure to comply with the Protocol on its own may not justify a costs
penalty or sanction, but it contributes to the overall picture of a party's
conduct of proceedings. Had the Defendant complied with the Protocol, in this case, maybe the Court would have been more understanding
about the failure to mediate?

In *Webb Resolutions Limited v Needham & Green (a firm)*, following settlement of a professional negligence claim, the Court was asked to
consider the position on costs and the defendant argued that the Court
should depart from the normal order for costs because the claimant had
failed to comply with the Professional Negligence Pre-Action Protocol
(the Protocol) by its unreasonable conduct in relation to disclosure.

The court had to make the normal order unless it considered it unjust
to do so and in deciding whether it was unjust, it had to take into
account all the circumstances of the case including the four matters
expressly set out in Rule 36.14(4).

The defendant argued that the Practice Direction for Pre-Action Conduct applied and in particular paragraph 4.2 (which provides that the
court expects the parties to have complied with this Practice Direction
or any relevant pre-action Protocol), paragraph 4.4 (which provides that
the court may decide there has been a failure of compliance because a
party has, without good reason, not disclosed documents requested to
be disclosed) and paragraph 4.6(2) (which provides that if, in the opinion of the court there has been non-compliance, the sanctions which
the court may impose include an order that the party at fault pays some
or all of the costs). Paragraph 4.5 is also relevant (it provides that the
court will look at the overall effect of non-compliance on the other
party when deciding whether to impose sanctions).

In cases where a party wants to settle a dispute at an early stage there is a tension between that party wanting to settle with minimum cost and inconvenience to himself and that party having to incur expense and effort in providing information to the other party so that other party might better inform himself about the dispute and his potential liability thereunder. Pre-Action protocols address that tension. CPR 36 also addresses that tension and provides a regime which prescribes an allocation of risk.

The aim of the Protocol (expressed in paragraph A2) is to establish a framework in which there is an early exchange of information so that the claim can be fully investigated and, if possible, resolved without the need for litigation. Paragraphs A4 and A5 make clear that the courts expect the parties to act reasonably and that sanctions will be imposed only if there is substantial non-compliance. The parties are urged to disregard minor departures from the Protocol and it is plain why that is so - the Protocol is urging a common sense approach to potential litigation, one that is practical and expedient and directed to an early resolution of the dispute at a proportionate cost.

The Court found that a claimant acting reasonably would, in the circumstances of this case, have supplied copies of the files at an early stage and not merely extracts therefrom. Instead of doing that the Claimant either refused without giving any good reason to supply the documents requested or failed to respond at all to the letters of request. Such conduct was not n accordance with the Protocol. It was not helpful or conducive to an early disposal of the case.

The Court was therefore satisfied that the claimant's non-compliance with the Protocol did make it unjust for the normal order under CPR 36.(10)(4) to flow. The claimant therefore had to pay the defendant's costs after the period when the disclosure should have been made.

However, in the case of Lincolnshire County Council v (1) Mouchel Business Services Limited (2) R.G. Carter Building Services Limited 13 February 2014 (a construction case), the Court rejected an application to extend time for service of a claim form on the basis that the parties had not complied with the Pre-Action Conduct Practice Direction and the Pre-Action Protocol for Construction & Engineering Disputes. The Claimant could have applied for directions. A party issuing proceedings to which the Pre-Action Protocol for Construction & Engineering Disputes applies without complying with the Protocol because his claim may become time barred is obliged under the Protocol to apply to the Court on notice for directions as to the timetable and form of procedure to be adopted. An application for directions on notice enables the Court to review the position in the light of any relevant submissions made by each affected party.

The Court accepted that the Protocol shows the importance attached by the Court to compliance with its requirements, but not that the Court's wish to ensure compliance with the Protocol is of paramount importance or in any way "trumps" the principles that are generally applicable to applications for extensions of time for the service of proceedings.

Pre-Action Protocol for the Resolution of Clinical Disputes

The original Clinical Negligence Protocol was introduced in 1998 ahead of, and anticipating, the CPR. The reason for the protocol was identified in para.1.1 of that protocol which stated:

> "The number of complaints and claims against hospitals, GPs, dentists and private healthcare providers is growing as patients become more prepared to question the treatment they are given, to seek explanations of what happened, and to seek appropriate redress. Patients may require further treatment, an apology, assurances about future action, or compensation. These trends are unlikely to change. The Patients' Charter encourages patients to have high expectations, and a revised NHS Complaints Procedure was implemented in 1996. The civil justice reforms and new Rules of Court should make litigation quicker, more user-friendly and less expensive."

The protocol continued:

> "It is clearly in the interests of patients, healthcare professionals and providers that patients' concerns, complaints and claims arising from their treatment are resolved as quickly, efficiently and profes-

sionally as possible. A climate of mistrust and lack of openness can seriously damage the patient/clinician relationship, unnecessarily prolong disputes (especially litigation), and reduce the resources available for treating patients. It may also cause additional work for, and lower the morale of, healthcare professionals."

On this basis the protocol went on to observe:

"If that mistrust is to be removed, and a more co-operative culture is to develop healthcare professionals and providers need to adopt a constructive approach to complaints and claims. They should accept that concerned patients are entitled to an explanation and an apology, if warranted, and to appropriate redress in the event of negligence. An overly defensive approach is not in the long-term interest of their main goal: patient care; patients should recognise that unintended and/or unfortunate consequences of medical treatment can only be rectified if they are brought to the attention of the healthcare provider as soon as possible."

The protocol then set out a process, with timescales, which provided for disclosure of health records, obtaining expert evidence, a letter of claim and a response. Subsequently, some minor modifications were made to the protocol, in particular extending time for the healthcare provider to respond to the letter of claim from three months to four months.

The 2015 Clinical Negligence Protocol

The updated Clinical Negligence Protocol came into effect on April 6, 2015. This version preserves the basic structure, and timescales, of the existing protocol but brings it up to date, reflecting other procedural changes, and makes some other modifications. Whilst not changing the context in which the protocol was first introduced the updated version, sensibly, omits much of that background and focuses more on the detail of the information that should be exchanged between the parties.

The scope of the protocol is confirmed by para.1.1 which states:

"This Protocol is intended to apply to all claims against hospitals, GPs, dentists and other healthcare providers (both NHS and

private) which involve an injury that is alleged to be the result of clinical negligence."

The protocol still expressly recognises the parties, as patient and health-care provider, may well have an ongoing relationship and hence para.1.3 states:

> *"It is important that each party to a clinical dispute has sufficient information and understanding of the other's perspective and case to be able to investigate a claim efficiently and, where appropriate, to resolve it. This Protocol encourages a cards-on-the-table approach when something has gone wrong with a claimant's treatment or the claimant is dissatisfied with that treatment and/or the outcome."*

It would appear that the word "perspective" was chosen to emphasise the importance of trying to clarify exactly what each party is actually trying to achieve (for example whether an apology and/or an explanation is going to be just as important as financial compensation) and to identify any misunderstandings that might prevent resolution (for example, a patient's interpretation of an entry in the medical records may be completely different to that of the clinician who wrote it)".

Objectives

Paragraph 2.2 identifies specific objectives of the Protocol.

1. Openness, transparency and early communication of perceived problems between patients and healthcare providers.

2. To help healthcare providers identify whether notification of a notifiable safety incident has been, or should be, sent to the claimant in accordance with a duty of candour under s.20 of the Health and Social Care Act 2008 (Regulated Activities) Regulations 2014.

3. Prompt disclosure of information to encourage early resolution or narrowing of the issues in dispute so healthcare providers can identify cases whether an investigation is required and involve the NHSLA or relevant defence organisation at an early stage.

4. Exploring mediation before issue of proceedings.

5. Identifying issues that may require a preliminary hearing.

6. Supporting efficient management of proceedings where litigation cannot be avoided.

7. Discouraging the prolonged pursuit of unmeritorious claims.

8. Discouraging the prolonged defence of meritorious claims.

9. Promoting rehabilitation.

10. Encouraging an early apology where appropriate.

Compliance and sanctions

The protocol now expressly reflects the importance attached to compliance with its terms and deals with sanctions that may be imposed in the event of default.

> *"This Protocol is now regarded by the courts as setting the standard of normal reasonable pre-action conduct for the resolution of clinical disputes."*

Consequently, para.1.7 explains:

> *"Where either party fails to comply with this Protocol, the court may impose sanctions. When deciding whether to do so, the court will look at whether the parties have complied in substance with the Protocol's relevant principles and requirements. It will also consider the effect any non-compliance has had on any other party. It is not likely to be concerned with minor or technical shortcomings (see paragraph 4.3 to 4.5 of the Practice Direction on Pre-Action Conduct)."*

ADR

Section 5 of the protocol deals with ADR, identifying the need to consider a number of different potential methods which are listed:

1. discussion and negotiation;

2. mediation;

3. arbitration;

4. early neutral evaluation; and

5. Ombudsman schemes.

Paragraph 5.4 provides that if court proceedings are issued the parties may be required to provide evidence that ADR has been considered and that, whilst recognising a party cannot be forced to enter any form of ADR, silence in response to an invitation to participate in ADR may be considered unreasonable and lead to the court ordering that party to pay "additional court costs".

The Pre-Action Protocol for Personal Injury Claims

The Personal Injury Protocol, like the Clinical Negligence Protocol, was introduced in 1998 anticipating the introduction of the CPR. The protocol, as it originally read, had a number of key features including the following.

1. A letter of claim, providing the defendant with information necessary to decide liability.

2. A time limit for the defendant to make a decision on liability.

3. Provision, where liability was admitted, for the defendant to be given information on quantum and then have a window in which to settle the claim, so as to avoid court proceedings.

4. Better provision of information, where liability was not admitted, so the claimant could properly assess the merits of any defence before incurring the costs of court proceedings, including reasons for any denial as well as any alternative case

5. The provision of documents relevant to liability.

6. Joint selection of experts (reflecting the intention of the Practice Direction—Pre-Action Conduct that the parties should try to agree a single expert, even if not a joint expert, wherever possible).

7. Clear timescales which if not met by the defendant would justify the claimant issuing court proceedings.

2015 Protocol

The revised PI Protocol, effective from April 6, 2015, contains a number of important changes to the original protocol.

Linkage with the RTA Protocol and the EL/PL Protocol

The PI Protocol remains significant even with the subsequent introduction of the Portal protocols, namely the RTA Protocol and the EL/PL Protocol. These new protocols are collectively now described in the PI Protocol as the "low value protocols" (although it is important to remember where claims start will not just depend on value but also the type of claim). Claims may enter the PI Protocol in a number of ways:

1. Claims which enter, but then leave a low value protocol will usually go into the PI Protocol.

2. Claims which might be suitable for a low value protocol in terms of value but are otherwise excluded will enter the PI Protocol from the outset.

3. Clams which are likely to exceed the relevant upper limit of a low value protocol (that is potential multi-track claims) will go straight into the PI Protocol.

Paragraph 1.1.1 of the PI Protocol makes clear that its terms do not apply while a claim is proceeding under a low value protocol.

The claim may have left the RTA Protocol or the EL/PL Protocol in circumstances where that protocol confirms Part 7 proceedings can be issued, which is reflected by the terms of para.1.2 of the PI Protocol. In other circumstances the claimant will need to have regard to the terms of the PI Protocol and the Practice Direction—Pre-Action Conduct to determine the stage at which Part 7 proceedings can be commenced.

Starting the claim

How the claim starts within the PI Protocol will depend on whether the claim is an ex-low value protocol claim or a non-low value protocol claim.

Links with the Low Value Protocol

Paragraph 1.3.1 of the PI Protocol confirms that where a claim exits a low value protocol because the defendant considers there is inadequate mandatory information in the claim notification form ("CNF") the claim will proceed on the basis the claimant must send a letter of claim in accordance with the PI Protocol.

In other circumstances para.1.3.2 confirms the claim will proceed under the PI Protocol on the basis the CNF will be treated as the letter of claim. The claimant may wish, even if a letter of claim is not required, to raise matters with the defendant that would have been raised in the letter of claim including disclosure, if liability is not admitted, and arrangements for expert evidence.

Paragraph 1.2 of the PI Protocol confirms that claims which exit a low value protocol prior to stage 2 will proceed on the basis of the terms of the protocol from which the claim has exited as well as the terms of the PI Protocol. The low value protocols specifically identify circumstances in which Part 7 proceedings can be commenced, and nothing in the PI Protocol should be seen as undermining those provisions.

Where the low value protocol does not expressly provide for Part 7 proceedings to be issued, the terms of the PI Protocol will determine when that is appropriate (important in such cases as these are likely still to be subject to fixed costs and hence a very important consideration is when the next stage in the costs matrix can be reached).

Starting the claim: Non-low value protocol

If a claim is not within the scope of either the RTA Protocol or the EL/PL Protocol, but is covered by the scope of the PI Protocol, a letter of claim, complying with the terms of the PI Protocol, should be sent at the outset.

<u>Settlement</u>

Paragraph 8.2 states that the parties should always consider whether it is appropriate to make a Pt 36 offer before issuing. As with the earlier version of the protocol the requirement is to "consider", rather than necessarily make, a Pt 36 offer at this stage.

Paragraph 9 deals specifically with ADR expressly identifying potential methods, and explaining what these mean, as the following:

1. Discussions and negotiation (which may or may not include making Pt 36 offers).

2. Mediation (a third party facilitating a resolution).

3. Arbitration (a third party deciding the dispute).

4. Early neutral evaluation (a third party giving an informed opinion on the dispute).

The protocol recognises that if proceedings are issued the parties may be required by the court to provide evidence that ADR has been considered.

<u>Compliance and sanctions</u>

Paragraph 1.5 of the PI Protocol confirms that where either party fails to comply with the terms of the protocol the court may impose sanctions and express reference is made to the terms of the Practice Direction—Pre-Action Conduct. Accordingly, as with the Clinical Negligence Protocol, sanctions may be applied by the court in the event of non-compliance. A defendant who ignores a claim or fails to respond in accordance with the terms of the relevant protocol is now clearly at risk of sanctions being imposed.

The added emphasis on the role of ADR in the protocols and accompanying practice direction is a further step towards the promotion of ADR over litigation, and the courts' use of sanctions where that approach is not followed

The pre-action protocols are, therefore, of real importance to both claimant and defendant personal injury practitioners.

Summary

- The pre-action protocols and the practice direction have been beefed up.

- Practitioners should follow the Protocols and engage in ADR or risk costs sanctions.

CHAPTER FIVE
THE PORTAL

Introduction

Low value injury claims present particular difficulties in relation to ADR as any process put in place must remain proportionate to the value of the claim. 2010 saw the introduction of a Pre Action Protocol focused on RTA claims worth under £10,000. In 2013, the present protocols were introduced. One is an updated version of the previous RTA process, and a second deals with employers' liability and public liability claims. Both extend to claims with a value of up to £25,000 and apply from 31 July 2013.

These protocols are the product of a Ministry of Justice consultation and assume claims information will be exchanged via an online portal. It is therefore common for claims proceeding under the protocols to be referred to as "MOJ" or "Portal" claims.

The protocols share the aims of ensuring:

> *"(1) the defendant pays damages and costs using the process set out in the protocol without the need for the claimant to start proceedings;*
>
> *(2) damages are paid within a reasonable time; and*
>
> *(3) the claimant's legal representative receives the fixed costs at each appropriate stage."*

In addition to these aims, the protocols and associated fixed costs rules have become a vehicle for government policy, particularly in relation to "reducing the number and cost of whiplash claims" [1].

Perhaps as a result of this, these protocols have received a significant amount of bad press, with criticism over high drop out rates, unfair costs and interference with access to justice. However, we suggest that

---

1 Ministry of Justice Consultation CP17/2012

these criticisms arise from the misconception discussed elsewhere that ADR is an additional hurdle prior to the litigation process. In fact, looked at on its own terms, we would suggest the protocols have proved immensely successful, allowing the settlement of around 1.4 million claims by August 2016[2], allowing parties and courts to focus their resource on the remaining, more complex cases.

In this section, we will discuss the two protocols together, as there are many similarities in the rules. In some sections, we will need to look in additional detail at rules applicable within one or other of the protocols or in relation to certain types of claim within a protocol, such as disease and whiplash.

In the subsequent chapter, we will see how claims can be referred for a judicial decision on quantum where parties fail to settle through the protocols.

References

For convenience, in this section we will use the following shorthand references:

- "RTA protocol" refers to the Pre-Action Protocol for Low Value Personal Injury Claims in Road Traffic Accidents from 31 July 2013

- "EL/PL protocol" refers to the Pre-Action Protocol for Low Value Personal Injury (Employers' Liability and Public Liability) Claims

- In this section "the protocols" refers to the RTA protocol and the EL/PL protocol together.

The Portal

"The Portal" is the online platform managed by Claims Portal Ltd to support the RTA and EL/PL protocols by allowing secure electronic

---

2 Claims Portal Ltd monthly MI, as published at www.claimsportal.org.uk

exchange of information, documents and offers between the parties. It has also become synonymous with the set of claims that fall within these protocols and are therefore required to be submitted through it, which are often referred to as "portal claims".

Legal service providers and Insurers who deal with these claims are expected to be registered to use the portal. They might set up their own staff as users of the portal, or can integrate the system with existing case management IT.

At the time of writing, use of the portal is free to claimant representatives as the system is paid for by the insurance industry. However, while insurers will continue to contribute towards the portal, it is anticipated that a charging system will be introduced whereby claimants will pay a low fee on submission of a claim.

Organisations who use the portal should have guidance and training in place for users, which reflects their own processes, therefore we will not describe the portal in detail. Portal Co also provide helpful user guides at www.claimsportal.org.uk/en/using-the-portal/

Practical Points

There are aspects of the protocols which are peculiar to them and which could pose traps for the unwary. Practitioners should be particularly mindful of the following:

- Information required to be exchanged by the protocol must be sent via the Portal (protocol 5.1, EL/PL protocol 5.1)

- Any communications not required by the Portal must be sent by email (RTA protocol 5.1, EL/PL protocol 5.1)

- Response times are counted in business days (any day excluding Saturday, Sunday, bank holidays, Good Friday or Christmas day) and time starts the business day after information which triggers the deadline was sent (RTA protocol 5.3 and 5.4, EL/PL protocol 5.3 and 5.4)

- Where the protocol gives a deadline for payment, the claimant must receive the cheque or the electronic transfer of funds before the deadline expires (RTA protocol 5.6, EL/PL protocol 5.6)

Scope of the Protocols

Each protocol includes detailed provisions in relation to their scope (RTA protocol 4.1, EL/PL protocol 4.1)

Between them, the protocols currently apply to the majority of personal injury claims worth between £1,000 and £25,000. In practice the rules on scope mean that the majority of injury claims fall within the process.

At the time of writing, a review of the small claims limit for injury claims is anticipated. The lower £1,000 threshold is currently set by reference to the small claims limit. It is unclear how a change to the small claims track may impact on the claims which fall within the protocols.

If it becomes apparent in the course of a claim that it is worth more than £25,000 then the claimant may notify the defendant and cause the claim to exit the process (RTA protocol 4.3, EL/PL protocol 4.2). Where it becomes apparent the claim is worth less, a claim may still be settled within the protocols but the claimant will only be entitled to the fixed costs associated with the protocol stage reached if the claimant reasonably believed at the outset that the claim was worth over £1,000 (RTA protocol 5.9, EL/PL protocol 45.9).

More specific rules as to scope are most conveniently considered according to claim type

Claims arising from RTAs.

"Road Traffic Accident" ("RTA") is defined as:

> "An accident resulting in bodily injury to a person caused by or arising out of the use of a mechanically propelled vehicle intended for use on roads, on a road (including any highway, road to which the public has access or bridge over which a road passes) or other

public place in England and Wales, unless the injury was caused wholly or in part by the defendant's breach of health and safety regulations enacted under s 53 of the Health and Safety at Work Act 1974." (RTA protocol 1.1)

In most circumstances, the definition ought to pose no difficulty, and this text is not the place to attempt a detailed examination of the scope of motor insurance law and its interface with employers' liability. However, it is worth noting developments at the European level[3] could lead to a change of scope, though anticipated exit from the EU leaves this highly uncertain.

In practice, where borderline cases involving a motor vehicle arise, it is submitted it would be prudent for a claimant to approach the motor insurer before commencing the portal process, inviting comment on use of the protocol within a reasonable period. This provides an opportunity for parties to use the protocol to facilitate settlement, and disputes as to costs may be avoided if applicability of the protocol is addressed at the outset.

In relation to RTAs, there are specific rules to be used in calculating the value of the claim, in order to determine whether it is with in the value limits of the protocol. The calculation should be carried out **excluding** the following "vehicle related damages" (RTA protocol 4.4 and 1.1 (18)):

- pre-accident value of the vehicle (in cases where the vehicle is a total loss)

- vehicle repairs

---

3 Damijan Vnuk v Zavarovalnica Trigalev (C-162/13) in which a farm labourer was injured by a reversing tractor on private property. The European Court of Justice concluded this was a situation in which the Slovenian Government ought, under the First Motor Insurance Directive, to have mandated motor insurance. If transposed into domestic law this would appear likely to broaden the scope of motor insurance to include private property and situations which employers may also be in breach of their duties.

- vehicle insurance excess

- hire of a replacement vehicle (including credit hire charges)

The reason for this exclusion is that these losses are often dealt with through direct negotiations between insurers and/or hire organisations so do not need to be considered under the protocol. This does not prevent a Claimant from including these losses in a stage 2 settlement pack, but even where the losses are to be included in this way, they do not contribute to the valuation used to assess whether the claim is within scope of the RTA protocol

Other exclusions relating to RTAs are set out at paragraph 4.5 of the RTA protocol. These are claims:

> "(1) In respect of a breach of duty owed to a road user by a person who is not a road user
>
> (2) made to the MIB pursuant to the Untraced Drivers Agreement 2003 or any subsequent or supplementary untraced Drivers' Agreements
>
> (3) where the claimant or defendant acts at the personal representative of a deceased person
>
> (4) where the claimant or defendant is a protected party as defined in rule 21.1(2) [of the CPR]
>
> (5) where the claimant is bankrupt; or
>
> (6) where the defendant's vehicle is registered outside the UK."

"Road user" in this context appears to be used loosely and to exclude, for example, claims arising from RTAs caused by a highway defect. It is clear from the definition of an RTA that accidents happening other than on a road are the subject of the protocol.

It is also worth noting that while protected parties are excluded from the process, children are not. Specific provisions exist to deal with approval of infant settlements.

EL (non disease) and PL claims

An employers' liability ("EL") claim is defined at 1.1(14) of the EL/PL protocol as

"a claim by an employee against their employer for damages arising from... a bodily injury sustained by the employee in the course of employment"

Disease claims (see below) are also categorised as EL claims.

A Public Liability (PL) claim is defined at 1.1(18) of the EL/PL protocol as:

"a claim for damages for personal injuries arising out of a breach of a statutory or common law duty of care made against:

(i) a person other than the claimant's employer

(ii) the claimant's employer in relation to matters arising other than in the course of the claimant's employment"

However, the definition of a PL claim excludes damages "arising from a disease...other than a physical or psychological injury caused by an accident or other single event."

As with motor claims, EL claims are generally simple to identify, though disputes as to the existence of an employment relationship and/or actions in the course of duty do sometimes arise. In practice this will often be academic in determining whether the protocol applies, as the PL definition serves to mop up the majority of injury claims not within the EL category.

A list of exclusions is set out at paragraph 4.3 of the EL/PL protocol, as follows (those specific to disease claims are dealt with in the next section):

"(1) where the claimant or defendant acts at the personal represent-ative of a deceased person

(2) where the claimant or defendant is a protected party as defined in rule 21.1(2) [of the CPR]

(3) in the case of a PL claim, where the defendant is an individual, (unless the individual is sued in their business capacity or in their capacity as an office holder)

(4) where the claimant is bankrupt

(5) where the defendant is insolvent and there is no identifiable insurer

(7) where the accident or alleged breach of duty occurred outside England and Wales

(8) for damages in relation to harm, abuse or neglect of children or vulnerable adults

(9) which includes a claim for clinical negligence

(10) for damages arising out of road traffic accidents"

EL Disease Claims

Disease claims come in many forms, including noise induced hearing loss, mesothelioma, other asbestos related conditions and claims for psychiatric conditions arising from stress. From the outset there has been debate as to the ability of the protocols to cater for such conditions, and as a result some specific rules have been included. However, it cannot be said that the protocols have been designed to cater for disease claims, and statistics indicate that under 12% settle within the process[4]

---

4 Portal Co MI August2016. Of c 50,522claims submitted to the portal, 19,695exited at stage 1, 827 at stage 2 and 23,471left as a result of the 'exit process' function (which covers a range of reasons). That indicates an exit rate of 88%. Only 2,373 (5%) have actually settled. The balance are still within the portal process, and may nor may not settle.

A "disease claim" within the protocol is defined as:

> *"a claim by an employee against their employer for damages arising from...a disease that the claimant is alleged to have contracted as a consequence of the employers breach of statutory or common law duties in the course of the employees employment, other than a physical or psychological injury caused by an accident or other single event."*

Disease claims fall within the wider category of an employer's liability claim. As is noted above, public liability disease claims are excluded, save those that arise from a single incident leading to bodily or psychological harm.

Unlike other categories of claim, disease claims arising from circumstances pre dating 31 July 2013 may be captured by the protocol. Disease claims will fall within the scope of the protocol where no letter of claim has been sent prior to 31 July 2013.

The general exclusions listed above in relation to EL and PL claims also apply to disease cases. In addition, the following are excluded by paragraph 4.3 of the EL/PL protocol:

> *"(6) claims where there is more than one employer defendant*
>
> *(10) mesothelioma claims"*

The Stages of the processes

The process under the protocols is divided into 2 stages:

- Stage 1 deals with issues of liability. Only where there is an admission of liability will a claim go on to:

- Stage 2 in which the claimant presents quantum evidence, the defendant responds and the parties attempt to negotiate settlement.

Claims which do not settle under the portal go on to the Stage 3 process, which is a referral to the Court for a decision on quantum, and is dealt with in the next chapter.

Before going on to look at the stages, it is worth looking at some of the preliminary steps that are either set out by the protocols or which may be useful in order to comply with the protocol requirements.

Preliminary steps

<u>Before the process begins</u>

We have already mentioned some circumstances in which it may be prudent to make contact with the defendant or their insurer before committing to the protocol process (or concluding it does not apply). This may avoid pitfalls in the course of the process, or unexpected disputes as to costs when it is concluded. Where disputes later arise, a party may find that such steps help them protect their position.

Therefore, while the protocols have nothing to say on the subject, there will be situations in which preliminary enquires are prudent. We cannot give exhaustive guidance, but these include:

- situations in which there is uncertainty as to the application of the protocols, such as where there may be a dispute as to whether an incident was on a road or other public place, or whether a PL claim is a disease claim.

- uncertainty as to the correct defendant. For example, where defective footway works lead to a PL claim, the identity of the responsible contractor in a chain of subcontractors may be unclear.

- uncertainty as to the relevant insurer. This arises most commonly in relation to PL claims. While the EL/PL protocol includes a process to be adopted where an insurer is not identified, the requirement that the claimant make a 'reasonable attempt' to identify an insurer (EL/PL protocol 6.1(3)) would seem to require some preliminary enquiries with the defendant and any insurers provisionally identified.

Dealing with limitation

The usual limitation period for injury claims is 3 years from the date of the incident giving rise to the claim [5], though there are a number of exceptions to the rule, which cannot be dealt with here.

Where it appears it will not be possible to complete the process under the protocols within the limitation period, a claimant is expected to commence Part 8 proceedings, as they would do upon commencing Stage 3. The claimant should apply to have those proceedings stayed pending completion of the protocol process by the parties (RTA protocol 5.7 and 5.8, EL/PL protocol 5.7 and 5.8).

In the event the claim proceeds through the process to stage 2, but does not settle, the claimant may apply to lift the stay and proceed with the stage 3 process.

Where liability is disputed, the claimant will similarly be able to apply to lift the stay, but in these circumstances will need to seek an Order allowing for filing of Particulars of Claim, with the claim to proceed thereafter as if it had been commenced under Part 7.

RTA Claims : askCUE PI

The askCUE PI service provides claimant representatives with access to information contained within the CUE database of injuries and illnesses reported to insurers.

Before commencing the protocol process in relation to an RTA claim, a claimant's representative must first undertake a search of askCUE PI, which will return a reference number to be inserted into the claims notification form. (RTA protocol 6.3A(1))

This step was inserted as a means of reducing fraudulent claims and it should go without saying that claimant representatives ought to take

---

5 Limitation Act 1980 s 11

advantage of results returned by askCUE PI in order to consider whether these raise any concerns as to the veracity of their client's claim before submitting the claims notification form.

If this is missing in the form first submitted, then a defendant may require the claimant to resubmit the form with the reference number included (RTA protocol 6.3A(2))

Stage 1

Content of the Claims Notification form ("CNF")

The submission of a claims notification form or "CNF" marks the beginning of the protocol process.

The CNF includes a number of mandatory questions which must be completed. Claimants should make a "reasonable attempt" to complete non-mandatory boxes. (RTA protocol 6.3, EL/PL protocol 6.3)

It should be borne in mind that the information within the CNF will form the basis of the defendant's investigation, so that providing good quality information is more likely to lead to the claim being resolved. Where a defendant considers the information to be inadequate, they may refuse to deal with the claim under the protocol, and costs sanctions may be applied by the Court. (RTA protocol 6.8, EL/PL protocol 6.7)

The protocols only provides for resubmission of the CNF in relation to a missing askCUE PI claim relating to an RTA claim. In all other cases, the protocols expect the form to be correctly completed when first submitted and costs sanctions may apply where this is not the case. In practice, the adequacy of information provided will often prove to be a grey area, and it will generally therefore be prudent for parties to attempt to engage with one another with a view to resolving ambiguities in the CNF prior to the deadline for the defendant's response.

The CNF includes a statement of truth. A claimant representative who electronically signs this prior to submission must be able to able to produce written evidence of authorisation to do so from their client (RTA protocol 6.6, EL/PL protocol 6.5).

RTA claims: vehicle related damage

Though quantum is generally dealt with at stage 2, the RTA protocol requires a limited amount of information to be provided at this stage in relation to vehicle related damage (RTA protocol 6.4).

If these are being dealt with by a third party, the CNF should say so. If they are being dealt with by the representative submitting the CNF then the CNF should confirm this and either attach relevant invoices or receipts or confirm when these are likely to be provided.

These provisions allow for rapid settlement of vehicle related damages where an admission is made (though they do not require the defendant to make any offer until stage 2).

Sending the CNF

The general rule is that the CNF is submitted to the defendant's insurer via the portal. At the same time, or as soon as practicable after that, a "defendant only" CNF (which excludes some personal information relating to the claimant) should be sent to the defendant (RTA protocol 6.1, EL/PL protocol 6.1(1)).

The requirement to additionally send a defendant only CNF to the defendant does not apply in a disease claim where the defendant is known to be dissolved, insolvent or to have ceased to trade.

Identifying the motor insurer

The RTA protocol proceeds on the assumption that where a vehicle is insured, identification of the insurer will not pose a problem. The Motor Insurance Database means that in practice this is generally reasonable.

Where there is no insurer, the MIB may be required to compensate the claimant, and the protocol includes provisions for claims under the Uninsured Drivers Agreement to be submitted to MIB via the Portal.

As is mentioned above, claims under the Untraced Drivers Agreement do not fall within the protocol.

<u>EL and PL claims : no insurer or no identified insurer</u>

It is more common for uncertainty over the identify of an insurer to arise in relation to EL and PL claims, and the EL/PL protocol therefore includes provisions to deal with these situations, and for claims in relation to which the defendant is not insured. These are set out at paragraph 6.1(2) and(3) of the EL/PL protocol

Where there is such uncertainty, a claimant must make a 'reasonable attempt' to identify an insurer. In relation to an EL claim, this must include a check of the EL Tracing Office (ELTO) database.

There is no advice as to what other steps may be required as part of a 'reasonable attempt' to identify an insurer, but as indicated above a letter to the defendant seeking the information will generally be expected. If the defendant has changed address or, in the case of a company, is no longer trading then further enquiries to establish a new address or contact receivers might form part of a 'reasonable attempt' .

Given the nature of the protocol, the limited costs available and the fact an alternative route for submission of the CNF is provided, it is our view that an extensive tracing exercise will not be required by the courts. However, it should be borne in mind that a claimant will often benefit from shorter response times and more certainty of having any award of damages satisfied if an insurer can be identified and involved in a claim at an early stage.

Where a defendant is known to lack insurance cover or (following reasonable attempts) the insurer cannot be identified, a CNF may be sent to the defendant's registered office or principal place of business.

If the defendant is in fact insured, then at the time of submitting an acknowledgement (see below), in accordance with paragraph 6.10 of the EL/PL protocol they must also send the CNF to the insurer and inform the claimant they have done so. The insurer must also send an acknowledgement to the claimant. Thereafter, the claimant must resubmit the CNF to the insurer via the portal as soon as possible or in any event within 30 days of the insurer acknowledgement.

Choice of insurer in relation to disease claims

Disease claims may relate to events or exposure over a period of time, and in that period an employer's insurers may have changed. Paragraph 6.1(4) of the EL/PL protocol states that the CNF should be sent to the insurer last on risk over the relevant period. (Note that as claims involving more than one employer are excluded from the protocol, provision is not made for this situation)

Acknowledgement

Both protocols provide for a defendant to send an electronic acknowledgement to the claimant the business day after receipt of the CNF (RTA protocol 6.10, EL/PL protocol 6.9)

However, the protocols contain no provision in relation to the consequences of a failure to acknowledge, and it has been held that failure to acknowledge under the earlier RTA protocol, which used identical wording to that of the EL/PL protocol, did not justify a claimant in discontinuing the portal process (*Patel v Fortis Insurance Ltd 5 December 2011*).

It is therefore suggested that while an acknowledgement no doubt amounts to good practice, a claimant who does not receive an acknowledgement ought not to take any further action unless and until the period for the response has elapsed.

Response

The defendant's response to the CNF must be submitted within the following period after the claimant submits the CNF:

RTA claims (other than against MIB)	15 working days	(RTA protocol 6.11)
RTA claims against MIB	30 working days	(RTA protocol 6.13)
EL claims	30 working days	(EL/PL protocol 6.11(a))
PL claims	40 working days	(EL/PL protocol 6.11(b))

Within the response, the defendant should set out whether liability is admitted or disputed. If admitted, the defendant should set out whether contributory negligence is alleged. If so, the defendant should set out brief reasons.

The claim will automatically leave the protocol if (RTA protocol 6.15, EL/PL protocol 6.13):

- the defendant does not respond within the above time limit

- liability is denied

- liability is admitted but contributory negligence is alleged, save where the contributory negligence arises in an RTA claim from the claimant's admitted failure to wear a seatbelt.

- The defendant responds to the effect that there is inadequate mandatory information in the CNF or the value of the claim is within the small claims track limit

The implications of a claim exiting the protocol are dealt with below.

In relation to RTA soft tissue injuries, rule 6.19A also permits the defendant to submit a version of events different to or in addition to the claimant's. This may, for example, provide information as to the speed of the impact. Where these details are provided by the defendant's insurer, the insurer must first obtain the defendant's written authority to provide the alternative account.

The content and status of an admission

An admission made under the protocols amounts to confirmation that (RTA protocol 1.1(1), EL/PL protocol 1.1(1)):

- a breach of duty occurred

- the breach caused some loss to the claimant

- the defendant has no defence under the Limitation Act 1980

In addition, in an RTA claim the admission amounts to confirmation that the accident occurred and was caused by the breach of duty .

CPR 14.1B limits a defendant's ability to withdraw its admission. In broad terms this may only be done where another party consents, or with permission of the court.

However, an exclusion to the binding nature of the admission is allowed in relation to causation. The defendant may withdraw its admission that the breach caused some loss to the claimant within the initial consideration period of stage 2 (CPR 14.1B(2)(a)). This allows the defendant to revisit the question of causation with the benefit of the medical evidence.

There is inconsistent caselaw in relation to the applicability of a portal admission to other claims. The issue typically arises in RTA claims, in which motorists A and B have been involved in a collision. Motorist A makes a claim, in relation to which motorist B's insurers make an admission via the portal. Is motorist B then bound by that admission in relation to his own injury claim?

In Ullah v John (20 March 2013) Parker DJ sitting in the Croydon County Court found that in these circumstances motorist B would be so bound. Having gone on to consider an application to resile from the admission, this was also refused. In *Malak v Nasim (10 December 2014)* Wood DJ, sitting in the Watford Country Court came to the contrary view that the insurer's admission in response to one claim did not bind their policyholder in relation to his own. In our submission, the latter approach is to be preferred, taking into account the policy behind the protocols. The Judge set out the argument as follows:

> *"There is no judicial decision made within the portal scheme and therefore there will not be two inconsistent judicial decisions: the most that can be said is that the Claimant's insurers decided to settle a claim brought by the Defendant in circumstances where, had liability been contested, they might have been successful in resisting that claim. The aim of the portal scheme is to provide a quick and cheap resolution, on the basis of a swift appraisal of the strengths of the case, without (in many instances) a full consideration of the merits. The possibility that a full examination of the facts might yield a different result does not detract from the desirability and utility of the scheme."*

Other scenarios might be identified in which this issue of the breadth of an admission might arise. For example, what of the claimant's passenger?

Each attempt to resile from an admission will be considered on its own circumstances, including the circumstances of the admission, timing of an application to resile and the availability of new evidence. Even taking this into account, there is, in our view, tension within the caselaw making this an area of particular uncertainty. The case of *Wood v Days Health UK Limited and others [2016] EWHC 1079 (QB)* provides an example of a claim in which an application to resile was dismissed. That application in part related to an increase in the claim's estimated value from £25,000 (though it was not within the protocols due to the incident date) to around £300,000, but issues of delay and prejudice also arose, leading the judge to the conclusion the admission should stand.

Defendants should therefore be aware that their admissions under the protocol are prima facie binding, and that the prospects of success in an application to resile may be uncertain. It would be prudent for defendants to consider making it clear that any admissions under the portal are limited to the claim presented, for example by accompanying them with an email to that effect. Challenges of new evidence arising after an admission or an increase in value of a claim will need to be considered on a case by case basis.

Medical Evidence

The collection of evidence by the claimant forms part of Stage 2 of the claims process, but as there are specific rules as to the evidence permitted, it is helpful to consider this as a separate exercise, normally undertaken following stage 1 and before submission of a Stage 2 pack.

Note that general rules on medical evidence are set out first below. Specific rules for soft tissue injury (whiplash) RTA claims are set out subsequently.

General Rules on medical reports

All claims will require at least one medical report to deal with the injuries sustained by the Claimant and the protocols suggest that in most cases one report will be sufficient to deal with the claim (RTA protocol 7.1 and 7.2, EL/PL protocol 7.1 and 7.2)

There is an assumption in the RTA protocol that in a claim worth less than £10,000 an expert will not need to see medical records (RTA protocol 7.5). No comparable assumption exists in the EL/PL protocol and it is suggested that it will often be prudent to obtain at least GP records in those cases, and all those over £10,000, in order to avoid the need for supplemental reports.

The protocol does not set out detailed rules as to the content of the report, though forms are available to experts and are often adopted in order to ensure a uniform approach. The expert is required to identify records reviewed for their report, and must set out details of records they consider relevant to the claim (whether provided or not). The claimant is required to disclose with the report those records that the expert states are relevant. (RTA protocol 7.4, EL/PL protocol 7.4)

Paragraph 1.1(12) of the RTA protocol and 1.1(16) of the EL/PL protocol define a medical expert as an expert registered with the General Medical Council or General Dental Council, or a psychologist or physiotherapist registered with the Health Care Professions Council. When instructing an expert to prepare a medical report, it should be assumed that such qualifications are required (though paragraphs 7.1 to 7.4 of the protocols could be clearer on this point).

Additional Medical Reports

Additional medical reports may be obtained where a claimant's injuries are such that an opinion of more than one specialist is required, based on the nature of the injuries (RTA protocol 7.2, EL/PL protocol 7.2). However, it should be noted that the protocols anticipate just one report in most cases, and a claimant might not recover the cost of an additional report if this is not reasonably required. Paragraph 7.31 of the RTA protocol and 7.29 of the EL/PL protocol requires the claimant to justify the cost of additional expert evidence in the Stage 2 Settlement Pack and provides the defendant with the opportunity to respond by refusing to pay and setting out reasons.

Subsequent medical reports

A 'subsequent' report is a second report from an expert who has already given an opinion. These must be justified and if they are not the claimant may not be able to recover the associated cost.

The rules (RTA protocol 7.8 EL/PL protocol 7.6) set out specific situations in which a subsequent report may be justified. Those are:

- the first medical report recommends that further time is required before a prognosis can be given

- the claimant is receiving ongoing treatment; or

- the claimant has not recovered in line with the original prognosis.

While the first and third justification are difficult to dispute, it is suggested that ongoing treatment may not, of itself, always be found by the courts to justify an additional report. If the treatment has been anticipated or recommended by an expert in an initial report, a prognosis given on the basis of the treatment, and the prognosis period remains good then it is difficult to see what a subsequent report has to offer. In such cases, it may be preferable to await conclusion of treatment and consider whether recovery has been achieved in line with prognosis before commissioning a subsequent report.

Where a subsequent medical report is to be obtained, the parties are expected to agree to stay the process for the necessary period (RTA protocol 7.12, EL/PL protocol 7.11) and an interim payment may be requested.

Soft tissue (whiplash) claims

The RTA protocol sets out specific rules in relation to medical reports in respect of these claims. Failure to follow the rules may mean the cost of a report is not recoverable.

A 'soft tissue injury claim' is defined as a claim "*brought by an occupant of a motor vehicle where the significant physical injury caused is a soft tissue injury and includes claims where there is a minor psychological injury secondary in significance to the physical injury*" (RTA protocol 1.1(16A))

Experts providing reports in such claims:

- must be instructed via the MedCo Portal at www.medco.org.uk ((RTA protocol 7.8A)

- may not have provided treatment to the claimant or be associated with anyone providing treatment (RTA protocol 1.1(10A)):

- must not propose or recommend treatment that is subsequently provided by them or by an associate (RTA protocol 1.1(10A)):

- must be registered with the General Medical Council, General Dental Council or be a psychologist of physiotherapist registered with the Health Care Professions Council (RTA protocol 1.1 (12))

If the defendant has provided a different version of events alongside their admission then this must be provided to the expert, and the expert must comment on the impact on diagnosis and prognosis on the basis of the claimant's account and on the basis of the defendant's account (RTA protocol 7.8A(2))

In relation to soft tissue injury claims, the claimant must first obtain a 'fixed cost medical report'. The claimant may only go on to obtain an additional or subsequent report where this is recommended within the fixed costs medical report and the fixed cost report has already been disclosed to the defendant. If the additional report is from an orthopaedic surgeon, A&E expert, GP or physiotherapist then it too must be a fixed cost report (RTA protocol 7.8B). The applicable fixed costs are set out later in this section

Other Evidence and Advice

Defendant's obligations

The evidence gathering exercise is generally a matter for the Claimant, but the EL/PL protocol requires that a Defendant to an EL claim provide "earnings *details to verify the claimant's loss of earnings, if any*" (EL/PL protocol 7.9). Typically this would be pay details beginning 13 weeks prior to the accident giving rise to the claim, to the conclusion of any period of absence. In some circumstances, such as where the claimant received overtime or similar additional payments that could have been affected by injury, then further records may be required.

Documentary Evidence

As set out above, where vehicle related damages are to be claimed, invoices and receipts should accompany the CNF or the CNF should state when they will be provided. The rules relating to medical reports also require disclosure of any records the expert considers relevant to the claim alongside the expert report.

There are no other specific rules in relation to the collection of evidence, but as the Stage 2 pack is expected to include all that is needed to value the claim, it is important that at the same time as obtaining medical reports, a claimant collects documentation in support of all pecuniary losses claimed.

Witness Evidence

The protocols state that witness statements 'will not generally be required' and there is no provision for the additional cost of obtaining statements, which will act as a disincentive to their preparation save where they are absolutely necessary. However, statements are allowed where 'reasonably required to value the claim'. (RTA protocol 7.11, EL/PL protocol 7.10)

It is anticipated that statements will only be required in order to support a head of loss not otherwise capable of being demonstrated. This may, for example, include a claim to gratuitous care or earnings that cannot be evidenced on disclosure alone (as where a self employed claimant was lining up a particularly lucrative contract).

Non medical expert evidence

This is also allowed 'where reasonably required to value the claim' but a claimant is at risk of being unable to recover the cost of the report if it is subsequently found not to have been 'reasonably required' (RTA protocol 7.9, EL/PL protocol 7.7)

In those cases where vehicle related damage is claimed, a valuer's report may fall within this category. In practice, other non medical expert evidence is rare in low value claims in any event, and so is unlikely to be 'reasonably required' in any but a few cases.

As for subsequent medical reports, where evidence is reasonably required the parties are expected to agree a stay (RTA protocol 7.12, EL/PL protocol 7.11). The protocol therefore appears to envisage parties exchanging views on the on the need for non-expert reports and the time required to obtain them.

Specialist legal advice

In relation to claims worth over £10,000, there is provision for specialist legal advice where reasonably required to value the claim, either from a specialist solicitor or from counsel, at an additional cost, equivalent to stage 3 type C costs, currently £150 (RTA protocol 7.10, EL/PL protocol 7.8 and CPR 45.23B).

However, the protocols expressly assume that in most cases the claimant's representative will be able to value the claim, and it is suggested that Courts will rarely be willing to allow the additional cost of such advice, in addition to the usual fixed fees.

The Stage 2 pack and negotiations

The Stage 2 pack

The pack should be submitted to the defendant within 15 working days of the claimant approving the final medical report or any non- expert report, whichever is later (RTA protocol 7.33, EL/PL protocol 7.31), though no sanction is set out for non-compliance and it is suggested that failure to comply ought not, in itself, to be seen as a significant breach of the protocol or to prevent the parties from continuing with stage 2.

The pack is intended to include all the information needed to value the claim. It should be noted that this will also form the basis of the pack submitted to the court in the event the claim is not settled, and so the claimant must set out his full case.

The stage 2 form requires the claimant to set out all heads of loss and details of disbursements together will full evidence in support, including medical and non medical expert reports, medical records or photographs accompanying reports, any witness statements, documents in support of pecuniary loss and evidence of disbursements (RTA protocol 7.32, EL/PL protocol 7.30).

In RTA cases where seatbelt related contributory negligence is alleged, the pack should include the Claimant's suggested percentage reduction (RTA protocol 7.34).

Stage 1 costs

Stage 1 costs are payable within 10 days of the Defendant receiving the Stage 2 settlement pack (RTA protocol 6.18, EL/PL protocol 6.16), save where the claimant is a child (in which case approval is required before any payments are made).

Costs at stage 1 are fixed, taking into account the type of claim (the value of the claim is considered irrelevant to liability costs). The sums payable are:

RTA claims   £200 (CPR 45.18 table 6)

EL/PL claims   £300 (CPR 45.18 table 6A)

In relation to soft tissue injury claims under the RTA protocol, the fixed cost medical report costs, and the cost of obtaining medical records are payable at the same time as the stage 1 costs, if the claimant has provided supporting invoices with the Stage 2 pack. Costs of the first fixed costs medical report are fixed at £180, while costs of medical records are capped at £80 (or £30 + the direct costs of the holder of the records, whichever is lower). These costs are set out at CPR 45.19 (2A), along with other fixed costs applying to medical evidence in soft tissue injury claims under the RTA protocol.

The Defendant's response

The defendant has up to 15 working days from receipt of the stage 2 pack to consider its contents and prepare a response. (RTA protocol 7.35 and 7.38, EL/PL protocol 7.32 and 7.35) If the defendant does not do so then the claim will no longer continue under the protocol.

It is open to a defendant at this stage to withdraw its admission of causation. If the defendant considers the claim to be worth less than the small claims track limit of £1,000, it may also give notice at this point.

If either of these occurs then the claim will leave the process. (RTA protocol 7.39, EL/PL protocol 7.36 and CPR 14.1B(2))

In most cases, the defendant will use this initial consideration period to consider and respond to the claimant's offer. It may accept the offer and thereby settle the claim (subject to approval if the claimant is an infant). More commonly, it will set out a response to the claim and a counter offer.

The response is entered on the Stage 2 pack. The Defendant has the opportunity to comment in relation to each head of loss claimed, and in doing so should bear in mind that if the claim does not settle this will form the basis of the Court's consideration of the case at stage 3.

The defendant will also make a counter offer. This may be the total of the sums put forward in relation to the individual heads of loss, or may be higher.

The defendant should also set out its response in relation to any disbursements it intends to challenge.

The "consideration periods"

The 15 day period for the defendant's response to the pack is known as 'the initial consideration period' but further time is afforded to ongoing negotiations. These are governed by provisions at paragraphs 7.35 to 7.37 of the RTA protocol and at 7.32 to 7.34 of the EL/PL protocol.

The 'total consideration period' is 35 days from the date the Stage 2 pack is submitted to the defendant, and all of the period following the defendant's response is intended for negotiations.

Both the initial consideration period and the total consideration period may be extended by the agreement of the parties.

The protocol does not provide for negotiations after conclusion of the total consideration period. However, if either party makes an offer within 5 days of the end of the period then the other has an additional 5 days after the end of that period in order to consider acceptance of the offer. Known as the 'further consideration period' this is intended to avoid either party being put under undue pressure by last minute offers.

<u>Withdrawal of offers</u>

Stage 2 offers may not be withdrawn within the consideration periods. Offers do not automatically lapse after the total consideration period (see *Purcell v McGarry heard by HHJ Gore in the Liverpool County Court on 7 December 2012)* but may be withdrawn once it has elapsed until stage 3 proceedings are commenced. If they are withdrawn in this way then the claim will exit the protocol (RTA protocol 7.46, EL/PL protocol 7.43).

Once stage 3 proceedings have started, an offer may only be withdrawn with the Court's permission, which will only be granted where there is 'good reason'. This is not explained but it is likely to require new evidence or information, for example undermining causation or suggesting exaggeration or fraud. However, if the Court grants permission then the claim will no longer continue under the Stage 3 process (Practice Direction 8B, paragraph 10.1).

<u>CRU</u>

The CNF includes information required for the Defendant to register a claim with the Compensation Recovery Unit in order to obtain a Certificate of Recoverable Benefits and, if relevant, a Certificate of NHS Charges.

The protocols state that the Defendant must apply for a certificate before the end of stage 1 (RTA protocol 6.12, EL/PL protocol 6.12) and in light of the strict time periods for negotiations, it will be important that Defendants ensure they keep an up to date certificate. Where the defendant makes a counter offer it is expected to indicate any sums in relation to recoverable benefits which are to be offset against the claim.

If a claim settles then the Defendant is expected to pay to the Claimant the sum of damages due, less any offsetable recoverable benefits, within 10 working days (see below). In he event that at the time of Stage 2 settlement the defendant does not have a certificate which will remain in force for the 10 day payment period, the defendant may apply promptly for an updated certificate, notify the claimant and make payment within 30 days of the end of the total consideration period (RTA protocol 7.49 and 7.50, EL/PL protocol 7.46 and 7.47).

Note that if, when dealing with Additional Damages under the RTA protocol (see the following chapter), the claim is settled but the Defendant has a CRU certificate which will expire within the payment period, a similar approach is taken (RTA protocol 7.63)

Stage 2 Settlement

Where a claimant is a child, approval is needed before any payments are made. Relevant provisions are considered in the chapter on Stage 3, which follows

In all other cases, payment of sums due to the claimant are to be made within 10 working days of settlement being agreed and should include (RTA protocol 7.47, EL/PL protocol7.44):

- agreed damages, less any deductible recoverable benefits or interim payment (see above in relation to a certificate of recoverable benefits which is about to expire at the time of settlement)

- any unpaid stage 1 costs, including the success fee on stage 1, if applicable

- stage 2 costs and disbursements, which are discussed further below.

Stage 2 costs

Save in claims by infants (which require approval) stage 2 costs are expected to be paid within 10 days of settlement of a claim. Note that by this point, stage 1 costs (excluding any success fee) will already have been paid. Costs comprise of the representative's fixed costs and disbursements.

The stage 2 fixed costs (payable in addition to the stage 1 costs) are determined based on whether the claim is under the RTA protocol or EL/PL protocol and on the value of the claim. The sums payable are:

RTA claims	valued at under £10,000	£300 (CPR 45.18 table 6)
	valued at £10,000 to £25,000	£600 (CPR 45.18 table 6)
EL/PL claims	valued at under £10,000	£600 (CPR 45.18 table 6)
	valued at £10,000 to £25,000	£1300 (CPR 45.18 table 6)

Disbursements that the claimant will seek to recover ought to be included within the Stage 2 settlement form, and invoices and fee notes ought to be included in the pack in support. The Defendant's response to the pack should include any objections to the disbursements claimed.

CPR 45.19 sets out details of those disbursements which can be recovered in relation to a claim that proceeds within the RTA or EL/PL protocol. Those are:

- The cost of obtaining medical records;

- The cost of a medical report or reports or non-medical expert reports as provided for in the relevant Protocol

- DVLA searches

- Motor Insurance Database searches

- Court fees where proceedings were started as a result of a limitation period that was about to expire (as set out above, in those circumstances, proceedings would be issued and stayed to allow the protocols to be followed)

- any other disbursement that has arisen due to a particular feature of the dispute

As set out above, where the value of the claim is over £10,000 and additional advice from counsel or a specialist solicitor is reasonably required to value the claim, the claimant may obtain such advice. The cost of doing so is fixed at £150 (CPR 45.23B).

Fixed disbursements in relation to soft tissue injury claims in the RTA protocol

In relation to soft tissue injury claims, additional rules govern recoverability of disbursements. Generally, no cost will be recoverable if the expert has provided treatment, is associated with a treatment provider, or proposes treatment that they or an associate subsequently provide (CPR 45.19 (2B)).

For fixed costs medical reports relating to soft tissue injury claims under the RTA protocol, medical report fees are fixed at (CPR 45.19(2A)):

For the first report:		£180
For a further report	if from an orthopaedic surgeon	£420
(where justified)	If from an A&E consultant	£360
	If from a registered GP	£180
	If from a registered physiotherapist	£180
Responses to Part 35 questions:		£80
an addendum report on medical records,		£50

other than by an orthopedic surgeon[6]:

The costs of obtaining medical records is capped at £80 or the direct cost from the holder plus £30 (whichever is less).

---

6 Save for an orthopaedic surgeon, whose report cost is taken to include such a review. See CPR 45.19 (2A)(b)(i)

Costs disputes

It is relatively rare for issues over the level of costs under the protocol to require court determination, as the rules are prescriptive as to the items which may be recovered. However, disputes do arise, most commonly in relation to the need for expert reports other than an initial medical report, and in relation to specialist advice.

Where there is a dispute at the end of Stage 2, the Defendant is expected to pay agreed damages and costs plus any sums offered for heads of loss not agreed, plus a sum it considers reasonable in relation to disputed disbursements following receipt of the court proceedings pack (see the following chapter). It is then anticipated that the court will determine all outstanding issues in relation to damages and costs during stage 3.

CPR45.29 also provides a mechanism for referral of costs disputes to the court where Stage 3 proceedings have already been commenced (see the next chapter)and then settle. In brief, either party may make an application to the court for determination of costs.

Interim Payments

The protocols set out a specific process by which claimants can request interim payments, and defendants may respond, with particular outcomes depending on whether payments are agreed or refused. These provisions do not apply where the claimant is a child – in such cases the claimant must commence a claim under CPR part 7 and make an application if an interim payment is required.

In order to request a payment, the claimant must provide an Interim Settlement Pack including an initial medical report and evidence of pecuniary loss (RTA protocol 7.14 and 7.15, EL/PL protocol 7.13 and 7.14).

It is immediately apparent from this that in many cases a claimant will not be able to request an interim payment until a point at which he or she has the evidence to prepare a Stage 2 pack, and so it will often be preferable to simply proceed with Stage 2 rather than invoking the interim payment process.

Request for a £1,000 interim payment

It is assumed that a £1,000 payment will generally be justified (as this is the lower value limit for claims under the protocols). Therefore, where the request is for £1,000, the Defendant is expected to make payment within 10 days of receipt of the interim settlement pack (RTA protocol 7.18, EL/PL protocol 7.17)[7].

If the Defendant fails to do so then the Claimant may remove the claim from the protocol, by giving notice within 10 days of the due date for payment and start proceedings under CPR part 7 (RTA protocol 7.28 and 7.30, EL/PL protocol 7.26 and 7.28)

Request for an interim payment over £1,000

Where the claimant seeks a sum of more than £1,000, the interim settlement pack must set out the heads of loss which are the subject of the payment (RTA protocol 7.16, EL/PL protocol 7.15). The Defendant has 15 days to consider the request and make a payment (RTA protocol 7.19, El/PL protocol 7.18).

Where the Defendant agrees the request then the full interim payment less any deductible benefits should be made within 15 days of receipt of the interim settlement pack.

Alternatively, the Defendant may make a lesser payment than the sum requested. The payment may not be less than £1,000 or the Claimant may remove the claim from the protocol by giving notice to the Defendant within 10 days of the due date for the response and payment, and may commence proceedings under Part 7 of the CPR (RTA protocol 7.28 and 7.30, EL/PL protocol 7.26 and 7.28). The Defendant must set out the reason for the reduced sum in the response sections

---

7 An exclusion applies for claims in respect of a disease to which the Pneumoconiosis etc. (Workers' Compensation) Act 1979 applies unless there is a valid CRU certificate showing no deduction for recoverable lump sum payments. See EL/PL protocol para 17.7(2)

of the interim settlement pack (RTA protocol 7.20 EL/PL protocol 7.19).

If the Defendant pays a reduced sum, and the claimant is not satisfied with the level of the payment, then the Claimant may still give notice of his or her intention to exit the protocol and thereafter commence Part 7 proceedings. However, if the interim payment awarded is no more favourable than that put forward by the Defendant then the claimants costs will be limited to those available had the claim settled at stage 2 (RTA protocol 7.29 and 7.30, EL/PL protocol 7.27 and 7.28).

Claims Exiting the protocols

As discussed above, there are a number of points at which claims might exit the protocols. Where this does occur, they revert to the more general pre action protocol processes or to litigation in accordance with CPR Part 7. Therefore:

- where at stage 1 the defendant notifies the claimant that the CNF includes inadequate mandatory information, the claim enters the pre-action protocol for personal injury claims at paragraph 5.1, requiring the claimant to submit a full letter of claim

- where the claim otherwise exits the process at stage 1, the claim continues from paragraph 6.3 of the pre action protocol for personal injury claims, with the CNF treated as if it were a letter of claim.

- In other circumstances, such as refusal of an interim payment, or where the defendant alleges the claim is within the small claims limit (in which case the personal injury pre action protocol will not apply) the claim may proceed directly to court proceedings under Part 7 of the CPR.

Once outside the protocol, claims cannot re-enter the process (RTA protocol 5.11, EL/PL protocol 5.11)

The potential sanctions associated with claims exiting the protocols should be noted. Each party runs a risk where a claim is allowed to exit the process.

Sanctions for non compliance

It is outside the scope of this book to discuss the broad range of sanctions available to the Court or the manner in which costs discretion may be applied so as to penalise procedural failings on the part of either party to a claim. This section is therefor limited to the main sanctions which are specific to the EL/PL and RTA protocol.

At the outset it should be noted that personal injury claims will be subject to qualified one way costs shifting ("QOCS"), limiting the circumstances in which a defendant can recover costs. Again, a discussion of QOCS is beyond the scope of this chapter but its impact is that the sanctions under the protocols are typically in the form of management of claimant costs.

Sanctions specific to the RTA and EL/PL protocol are built in to the associated fixed costs regime.

We have already seen that in relation to soft tissue injury claims, the cost of an expert report may be refused if it does not comply with rules excluding the reporting expert or associates from providing treatment.

We have also discussed the fixed costs applicable to claims under the protocols and restrictions on recoverable disbursements which, while not a sanction, limit the costs a claimant may recover in the event they go beyond the scope of enquiries envisaged by the protocols.

However, significant failures to comply with the protocol generally lead to claims exiting the process. The sanctions regime manages this behaviour by setting out rules as to whether the fixed costs under the protocol should or should not be applied.

CPR 45.24 (1) and (2) therefore states that where a claimant does not comply with the protocol or elects not to continue with the protocol, the court may nonetheless limit costs to the fixed costs which would have applied to the claim had it been pursued under the relevant protocol if:

- The claimant provided insufficient information in the CNF, leading to the defendant refusing to proceed with the process; or

- The claimant acted unreasonably by discontinuing thee protocol process; or

- The claimant acted unreasonably in valuing the claim at more than £25,000 thereby excluding it from the protocol process; or

- The claimant did not comply with the protocol despite the claim falling within its scope

This amounts to a sanction as the costs the claimant is in fact likely to incur in pursuing the alternative pre action protocol and Part 7 claim would typically be higher than the costs incurred through the RTA or EL/PL protocol process and the claimant will be left to bear the difference.

Similarly, where a claimant starts proceedings for an interim payment, the defendant having refused to pay the sum requested through the protocol process (discussed above), the claimants costs may nonetheless be limited to protocol costs if the payment awarded is no more than that the defendant was prepared to make under the protocol process (CPR 45.24(3)).

In relation to soft tissue injury claims under the RTA protocol an additional sanction is applied where a claimant has failed to enter the mandatory information from askCUEPI on the CNF and then fails to resubmit the CNF when requested to do so by the Defendant in accordance with 6.3A(2) of the RTA protocol. In those circumstances, CPR 45.24(2A) states the court may not order the defendant to pay the claimants costs and disbursements at all, save in exceptional circumstances.

It is worth noting at this point the position in relation to small claims. Small claims costs under the first part of CPR 45 are typically lower than those under the protocol process. Therefore where a small claim exits the process and is resolved through small claims proceedings, costs may be less. The claimant is protected where they reasonably believed the value of the claim to be over £1,000 when commencing the portal process by paragraph 5.9 of the RTA and EL/PL protocols which permit them to recover stage 1 and, where applicable, stage 2 costs.

For defendants, management of non-compliance are also costs based, but in these cases, the 'sanction' is typically the increased costs that the claimant may recover when a claim exits the protocol through no fault on the part of the claimant.

Resolving claims that do not settle

We will discuss the steps taken to deal with those claims that have proceeded to the end of Stage 2 without settlement in the following chapter.

Summary

- The RTA protocol and EL/PL protocol set out processes for settlement of injury claims valued between £1,000 and £25,000.

- The process uses standardised forms exchanged via an online portal in accordance with strict rules and time limits for parties to exchange information, evidence and offers.

- Additional rules apply to soft tissue (whiplash) injuries arising from an RTA.

- Claims will leave the protocol where there is a liability dispute or an allegation of contributory negligence (save under the RTA protocol in relation to a claimant's admitted failure to use a seatbelt).

- Where liability is admitted, the process allows the claimant to prepare a settlement pack in relation to quantum, with a negotiation process aimed at settling the claim thereafter.

- A specific regime of fixed costs and recoverable disbursements applies to the process.

- Sanctions, generally in the form of additional costs exposure for defendants or restricted costs recovery for claimants, apply where a party fails to comply with the process.

CHAPTER SIX
STAGE 3 HEARINGS

Resolving claims not settled in stage 2

Where low value personal injury claims that are subject to the protocols discussed in the previous chapter have reached the end of stage 2 without settlement, stage 3 allows for a judicial determination of quantum, at minimal cost.

However, before this can take place a number of steps must take place. This chapter will deal with what happens to a claim that has not settled by the end of stage 2.

RTA Claims: Vehicle Related Damages

It will be recalled that "vehicle related damages" (discussed in more detail in the previous chapter) need not be included in a Stage 2 settlement pack. However, if a claim is to become subject to a judicial decision than all elements of loss need to be dealt with together. Therefore the RTA Protocol includes a process to achieve this.

The stage 2 form with Additional Damages

The RTA protocol uses the terminology "original damages" to refer to all losses included in the Stage 2 settlement pack and "additional damages" to refer to any other vehicle related damages which have not settled by the end of Stage 2 (RTA protocol 7.51).

Where this situation arises, the claimant must notify the Defendant that there are additional damages to be considered, obtain relevant information on those damages (which will usually be held by an insurer or credit hire organisation) and then amend the Stage 2 settlement pack form to include these losses and an updated offer which takes them into account (RTA protocol 7.52)..

Note that other changes to the Stage 2 form are not permitted at this stage. So, for example, the Claimant is not permitted to introduce new losses other than vehicle related damages.

The Defendant then has 15 working days to agree the claimant's offer or make a counter offer. If a counter offer is made then reasons for any reduction in the additional damages claim must be set out (RTA protocol 7.53-54).

Settlement of all or part of the claim prior to the stage 3 claim form

The rules in this regard are set out at 7.55-56, 7.59-60 and 7.62 of the RTA protocol

Where a claimant is a child, approval is needed before any payments are made. Relevant provisions are considered below.

In all other cases, where the original damages are settled at this stage, payment of sums due to the claimant are to be made within 10 working days of settlement being agreed.

The payment(s) should include:

- agreed damages, less any deductible recoverable benefits or interim payment

- any unpaid stage 1 costs, including the success fee on stage 1, if applicable

- stage 2 costs and disbursements, which are discussed in the preceding chapter.

- any late settlement costs due (see below)

If additional damages and original damages have been settled at this stage (or there were no additional damages) then the agreed damages will include both and the whole claim will be concluded. The defendant will additionally be required to pay "late settlement costs" if the settlement is greater than the offer made in response to the stage 2 pack with additional damages (under 7.53) and the court proceedings pack has been sent to the defendant before settlement (RTA protocol 7.56 and CPR 45.23A)

If only the original damages have been settled then these will be the only agreed damages to be paid. However, the additional damages will still need to be dealt with. The additional damages claim cannot proceed through the stage 3 process (as it is not a personal injury claim) but it remains open to the Claimant to commence a Part 7 claim in relation to those losses.

Where the additional damages are agreed, but the original damages are not, then the amount of the additional damages must be paid within 10 working days of agreement. The remaining elements of the claim will be dealt with as described below (RTA protocol 7.58).

The Court Proceedings Pack

EL and PL claims and those RTA cases where there are no outstanding vehicle related damages at the end of the Stage 2 consideration periods can proceed straight to the court proceeding pack stage, once the Stage 2 consideration periods have elapsed (RTA protocol 7.64, EL/PL protocol 7.48)

As discussed above, some RTA claims will need to proceed through an additional process in order to bring all heads of loss together before proceeding to this stage, but if the 'original damages' elements do not settle, then the Court Proceedings Pack is the next step.

The Court proceedings pack is comprised of two forms. Part A sets out all losses claimed by the claimant (including additional damages, where relevant in an RTA protocol claim) in much the same format as the stage 2 settlement pack. It also includes the Defendant's proposed valuations of losses, and comments in support. Parties may not raise anything not already raised in the Stage 2 form (RTA protocol 7.66,

EL/PL protocol 7.49). This document is accompanied by evidence exchanged by the parties in support of those losses.

Part B of the pack sets out the final offers made by each of the parties within the stage 2 consideration periods. This is kept separate from Part A so that the Judge deciding the claim can review the offers only when it comes to deciding on the award of costs.

The claimant must first provide a copy of the pack to the Defendant who then has 5 working days to check the pack to ensure it contains the correct information, and to nominate solicitors for service of subsequent proceedings. If the Defendant does not respond within 5 working days then the Claimant may assume the pack is agreed (RTA protocol 7.67-7.69, EL/PL protocol 7.50 – 7.52).

Payment following Court Proceedings Pack

Unless the claimant is a child, the Defendant must pay to the claimant as much of the damages and costs as is not disputed within 15 working days of receiving the Court Proceedings Pack. This includes (RTA protocol 7.70, EL/PL protocol 7.53):

- the final damages offer made by the defendant (as set out in the Court Proceedings Pack), less any deductible benefits or interim payments.

- any unpaid stage 1 costs

- stage 2 fixed costs

- stage 2 disbursements that are not disputed. If the amount is disputed, the Defendant must pay as much as it considers reasonable (RTA protocol 7.71, EL/PL protocol 7.54).

As for other payments under the protocol, if the certificate of recoverable benefits will remain in force for less than 10 days when the pack is received, the claimant must be advised, a certificate sought, and payment made within 30 days of receiving the Court Proceedings Pack (RTA protocol 7.73 – 7.75, EL/PL protocol 7.56-7.58).

If the Defendant fails to make these payments, the claim will exit the Protocol Process.

The Stage 3 Process

Stage 3 utilises the "Part 8" process within the Civil Procedure Rules to bring a claim before the court either for determination of quantum, where the parties have been unable to settle, or for the purpose of having an infant settlement approved. The rules are set out at Practice Direction 8B.

The Start of stage 3

Stage 3 commences (and stage 3 costs begin to apply) when the claim form and accompanying documents are filed with the court (practice direction 8B paragraph 6.2)

The Claim Form

We have already discussed the process by which the Court Proceedings Pack is prepared by the Claimant, and this will form the basis on which the Court will consider the claim.

Therefore the information required within the Part 8 claim form is limited to (Practice direction 8B, paragraph 5.2):

- A statement that the claimant has followed the relevant Protocol

- Dates to avoid where a hearing is requested or the Claimant is a child

- The value of the claim

and, where the claim is not for the purpose of approval of a claim for an infant:

- The date the court proceedings pack was sent to the Defendant

- Whether the claimant wants the court to determine the matter on the papers, without a hearing.

Note that where the defendant is uninsured and MIB have consented to be joined, they should be included as second defendant to the claim (Practice direction 8B paragraph 6.6).

<u>Documents accompanying the claim form</u>

It is assumed that evidence has already been exchanged in compliance with the protocol, and the parties are not permitted to introduce new arguments or new evidence at stage 3. Therefore the process is designed to ensure that at the same time as filing and serving the claim form, the claimant files and serves relevant evidence. If evidence is not filed and served with the claim form then it may not be relied on.

In all cases, the following should be filed and served with the claim form (Practice direction 8B paragraph 6.1):

- Court proceedings pack part A form

- Copies of medical reports (in the case of whiplash claims, this should include at least one fixed cost medical report – see the preceding chapter)

- Evidence in support of special damages

- Evidence in support of disbursements.

- Where the Defendant is uninsured and MIB have consented to be second defendant, their CNF response form.

In relation to stage 3 claims that are not for approval of an infant settlement, the claimant should also file and serve:

- Court proceedings pack Part B

Additional documents to be provided in infant approval claims

In addition the above, the following should be filed and served in relation to a Stage 3 claim for the purpose of approval of an infant settlement (practice direction 8B paragraph 6.5):

- A draft consent order

- advice by counsel, a solicitor or other legal representative on the amount of damages

- A statement of the litigation friend confirming recovery in accordance with the prognosis and detailing any ongoing symptoms, with a signed statement of truth.

Further Evidence

The stage 3 process is not designed to deal with the introduction of new evidence, though there is scope for the court to permit it and give directions for exchange under paragraph 7.1(3) of practice direction 8B

However, paragraph 7.2 requires the court to transfer the case to the Part 7 process, allocate it to a track and give directions where it appears further evidence should be provided and the claim is not suitable to continue under the stage 3 process. In practice where directions are required it is often likely to be concluded that the claim is therefore unsuitable for the stage 3 process leading to this result. In such cases, Stage 3 fixed costs will not be allowed (PD 7B, paragraph 7.3).

Acknowledgement of Service

A specific form (N201B) is available for the acknowledgement. This may be completed by the insurer, who may also give their address for the purpose of service (Practice direction 8B, paragraph 8.5)

The Acknowledgement must state whether the Defendant contests the amount of damages, contests any award of damages, disputes the court's jurisdiction or objects to use of the stage 3 process (Practice direction 8B, paragraph 8.3).

If there is an objection to use of the stage 3 process then the reasons should be given (Practice direction 8B, paragraph 8.4). The claim will be dismissed if the reason is that the Claimant has failed to follow the protocol or has filed new evidence. In these circumstances, the Claimant may commence fresh proceedings under Part 7 (Practice direction 8B, paragraph 9.1), though costs consequences may apply.

The acknowledgement also permits the Defendant to request an oral hearing or a decision on the papers (Practice direction 8B, paragraph 8.3).

Oral hearing or Decision on the papers

If the claim is for approval of an infant settlement, an oral hearing will be listed. In other cases, an oral hearing will be listed if requested by either party or if the Court considers this appropriate (Practice direction 8B, paragraph 11.1).

In either case, the Court will give at least 21 days notice of the hearing or determination date, and if additional deductible benefits have accrued the Defendant must file the up to date Certificate of Recoverable Benefits at least 5 days before the hearing.

The process at the hearing

As all evidence ought to have been provided to the court within the Court Proceedings Pack, and the parties have set out their arguments in writing, a Stage 3 hearing will typically be listed for 10 minutes only.

Witness evidence is rare in the process, and even if used, witnesses will not generally be expected to give evidence at the hearing. Brief submissions might be made, drawing attention to key points in the evidence and caselaw in support of general damages before the Judge makes a decision on the sum to award.

Only once damages are assessed will the Judge refer to Part B of the Court Proceedings Pack. This will provide information as to the parties' offers and allow the Judge to determine the appropriate costs award (see below). There may be further submissions if there is a dispute as to whether disbursements should be allowed, or as to the sum to be awarded in relation to disbursements.

The court will grant an order setting out both the sum to be paid in relation to damages and the sum awarded in relation to costs, with a period for payment (typically 14 or 21 days)

Settlement during stage 3

A significant number of claims are settled after stage 3 has commenced. Specific costs rules (see below) cater for this situation.

If the Claimant is a child and settlement is achieved during stage 3, then an application may be made to use the Stage 3 hearing for the purpose of approval. The Claimant will need to file with that application the additional documents required in relation to infant approval claims (see above).

Additional Rules for Infant claims

The above process is also used for the purpose of approval of infant claims settled at stage 2 or early in stage 3. Modifications to the process which apply to these claims are set out in the relevant sections above.

The Judge will typically want to hear from the litigation friend at an approval hearing, and my ask the child questions (depending on their age and ability to deal with this). However, this is undertaken in an informal manner and (save for the requirement for a statement in relation to prognosis from the litigation friend) does not need to be anticipated with detailed statements.

If approval of a settlement achieved at stage 2 cannot be granted at the first Stage 3 hearing, but the Judge considers the matter can be resolved through the stage 3 process then a second approval hearing may be listed, though only 2 hearings are permitted as part of the stage 3 process (Practice direction 8B paragraph 12.3 and 12.5). In practice this gives the parties the parties the opportunity to address any concerns raised by the Judge which have prevented approval at a first hearing.

If settlement is achieved at stage 3 the claimant may apply for the court to approve the settlement. If the application is not granted then the Court will order the claim to proceed to a stage 3 hearing for a determination of quantum (Practice direction 8B paragraph 13.3)

If the Judge considers the process is not appropriate (for example due to a need for additional evidence) or if the claim is not approved at the second hearing, then the claim will leave the process and the Judge will give directions for its future conduct (practice direction 8B paragraph 12.4 and 12.5).

Costs at stage 3

Stage 3 is also subject to a fixed costs regime set out in section III of CPR 45. Stage 1 and 2 costs and disbursements are discussed in the previous chapter. By the commencement of stage 3 the majority of stage

1 and 2 costs and disbursements are expected to have been paid. This section therefore focuses on the costs specifically associated with stage 3

Stage 3 costs are divided into three elements, as follows (CPR 45 table 6 and 6A):

- Stage 3 type A: £250

- Stage 3 type B: £250

- Stage 3 type C: £150

Recoverable disbursements are limited under the fixed costs regime. Details of recoverable disbursements are set out in the preceding chapter. In addition at stage 3 recovery of court fees associated with issuing the Stage 3 proceedings may be recovered.

Costs on settlement at stage 3

Where the parties settle following commencement of stage 3 proceedings, and the settlement sum is less than or equal to the defendants protocol offer, the defendant must pay outstanding stage 1 and stage 2 costs and disbursements recoverable under the fixed costs regime (CPR 45.25(3)).

Where the parties settle following commencement of proceedings and the settlement sum is more than the defendant's protocol offer, the defendant must pay outstanding stage 1 and stage 2 costs, plus stage 3 type A costs, plus disbursements recoverable under the fixed costs regime (CPR 45.25(2)).

Costs following judgment in a sum equal to or less than the defendant's protocol offer

Where the court determines damages (either at a hearing or on the papers) the Judge will then consider the offers made by each party by looking at part B of the court proceedings pack

Where the claimant has failed to do better than the defendant's protocol offer, the claimant will still retain stage 1 and stage 2 costs and disbursements, but will not receive stage 3 costs.

The claimant will, however, be ordered to pay to the defendant stage 3 type A costs and, where an oral hearing has taken place, stage 3 type B costs (CPR 45.26)with interest from the first business date after the date the court proceedings pack was sent to the defendant (CPR 36.29)

Costs following judgment in a sum between the claimant and defendant's protocol offers

Where damages are assessed as being greater than the defendant's offer but less than the claimant's, the defendant will be required to pay the claimant the stage 3 type A fixed costs, and where an oral hearing has taken place, type B fixed costs in addition to any outstanding stage 1 or 2 costs and disbursements. (CPR 36.29 and 45.20)

Costs following judgment in a sum greater than the claimant's protocol offer

In this situation, the defendant will be required to pay the claimant the stage 3 type A fixed costs and, where an oral hearing has taken place, type B fixed costs in addition to any outstanding stage 1 or 2 costs and disbursements. In addition the court must order the defendant to pay interest on those costs at a rate not exceeding 10% above base rate (CPR 36.29 and 45.20)

Costs in infant approval claims

An approval hearing will not involve judicial determination of the claim value, as this will already have been settled. Costs will depend upon the circumstances of the settlement and whether more than one hearing is required before settlement. Relevant rules are set out at CPR 45.21 and 45.22.

An oral hearing will be required in order for the court to approve the settlement, and the court will need to be provided with an advice on the settlement as part of the bundle filed prior to the hearing. Therefore in addition to stage 1 and 2 costs and disbursements, the defendant will generally be required to pay the claimant stage 3 type A, B and C fixed costs.

Where a second hearing is required before the settlement is approved then the court has an additional discretion to require either party to pay type A and/or type B fixed costs to the other. Though not clearly specified, the discretion can be expected to be exercised in the defendant's favour only where there has been some fault on the part of the claimant resulting in the need for a second hearing.

Where at a stage 3 hearing the court concludes the claim is not suitable to be determined via the stage 3 process then the court will order the defendant to pay any outstanding stage 1 and stage 2 fixed costs as well as stage 3 type A, B and C fixed costs (CPR 45.23)

Consequences of a protocol offer following judgment

These are dealt with under CPR 36. 24 to 36.29. A significant consequence of the offer will typically be in relation to the costs order made, and this is discussed in the section immediately above.

However, additional consequences apply where the judgment is for a sum greater than the claimants offer. In these cases, in addition to the costs consequences set out above, the court must order the defendant to pay (CPR 36.29):

- An additional sum calculated as 10% of the amount of damages awarded

- Interest on damages at a rate of up to 10% above base rate for some or all of the period from the first business day after the court proceedings pack was sent to the defendant

Summary

- Stage 3 provides a process for the Court to determine quantum where parties have not been able to do so via stages 1 and 2 of the portal process discussed in the previous chapter.

- There are a number of steps which must be taken following conclusion of the negotiations phase of Stage 2 and before the commencement of stage 3 proceedings. In particular in claims under the RTA protocol, additional damages must be considered.

- There remains an opportunity to settle during the preparations for stage 3 and following commencement of stage 3 proceedings. However, additional costs will be incurred and it is therefore preferable to settle during stage 2

- Fixed costs apply to stage 3

- Where one party fails to better the other's protocol offer, it can expect to be subject to penalties in terms of the costs order, interest and (where a claimant receives more than his or her protocol offer) an additional award on damages.

- Stage 3 also provides a process by which approval of infant claims settled at stage 2 or Stage 3 may be secured.

CHAPTER SEVEN
PART 36 AND
SETTLEMENT OFFERS

Pitfalls and Part 36 offers

Parties to litigation are firmly encouraged to consider how best to settle disputes and to use all the necessary tools available including using Part 36 offers. Given the cost protection which flows from a Part 36 offer, these have great importance. However various criticisms have been made by practitioners and Judges alike about various aspects of the Rule. As a result the Civil Procedure Rule Committee (CPRC) appointed a sub-committee to review Part 36 resulting in various amendments which came into force in April 2015.

Offers of Settlement in the Litigation Process

CPR r.36.2(2) provides: "Nothing in this Section prevents a party making an offer to settle in whatever way that party chooses, but if the offer is not made in accordance with rule 36.5, it will not have the consequences specified in this Section."

The rule contains a reminder that CPR r.44.2 requires the court to consider an offer to settle that does not have the costs consequences set out in this section in deciding what order to make about costs. Where the consequences of a Pt 36 offer do not apply that may be important to the claimant, as there will not be the added certainty of deemed costs provisions, and will also be significant if the offeror seeks to rely on the offer for costs purposes because, away from CPR Pt 36, there will be no "automatic" consequences: Widlake v BAA Ltd [2009] EWCA Civ 1256; [2010] C.P. Rep. 13; Saigol v Thorney Ltd (t/a Thorney Motorsport) [2014] EWCA Civ 556; [2014] 4 Costs L.O. 592.

Offers within litigation generally fall within the following categories:-

1. An open offer

This is made without the privilege associated with the without prejudice rule.

The advantage of making such an offer is that it be used to demonstrate to the Court that the offeror was acting reasonably in the proceedings. The disadvantage is that the terms of the offer may be disclosed to the Court and may influence the Court's view on a party's position.

These are a good tool to use when parties feel like their opposition are being overly optimistic about the outcome of the case and there is virtually no possibility of the offer being better at trial.

2. Without prejudice offersThese fall into two categories.

A Calderbank offer, also known as offers made "without prejudice save as to costs", which are usually contained in a letter marked with this phras, meaning they may not be referred to in the main proceeidngs but may be on the matter of costs. While offers made on these terms will carry some weight with the Court when it comes to the decision of costs they do not carry the same consequences as Part 36 offers.

A without prejudice offer (note the exclusion of 'save as to costs')cannot be referred to on the issue of costs, in the main proceedings or subsequently save for in a few exceptional circumstances.

Both forms of without prejudice offers are useful if a party wants to make an offer to settle for a sum which is inclusive of costs and the level of the offer made in respect of costs will probably the factor which determines whether the offer is made with full without prejudice status or whether it is made without prejudice save as to costs.

3. Part 36 offers

This is an offer to settle made in accordance with CPR 36.5 and which will attract the consequences in respect of costs and interest set out in CPR 36.13, 14 and 17.

Making a Part 36 offer is one of the most important tactical steps a party can take during the course of legal proceedings

Part 36 provides a means of putting pressure on your opponent to settle a case and to some extent provides you with some protection in respect of your costs

If your opponent does not accept your Part 36 offer then that party takes a significant risk as to costs and interest. This means that at the same time you must also give careful consideration to any Part 36 offers made by your opponent.

Because of this you need to consider Part 36 offers at all key stages of the litigation process whether it be making one, accepting one, withdrawing one or revising one.

Requirements of Part 36 Offers

It is the specific way in which the offer is made which sets a Part 36 offer apart from any other offer to settle. Because of their technicalities the rules relating to Part 36 have historically been the subject of extensive case law. On 6 April 2015 the Civil Procedure (Amendment No 8) brought into force a revised Part 36 which was intended to clarify, simplify and codify some of the most significant case law relating to Part 36 into the rules.

In order to trigger the consequences of Part 36 the offer made must be comply with CPR Part 36.5 (new provisions) which means that it must be:

- made in writing

- make it clear that the offer is made pursuant to Part 36

- specify the relevant period

- state whether it relates to the whole of the claim, to part of the claim or to an issue that arises in it and if so to which part or issue. When making an offer on this basis it is important to exercise care to make sure the part of the claim or which particular issue the offer relates to is clearly defined.

- state whether it includes any counterclaim. Counterclaims are treated as claims for the purposes of Part 36 and so in cases which involves counterclaim parties need to expressly state whether an offer includes the counterclaim

Timing of the offer

- CPR r.36.7 confirms a Pt 36 offer can be made at any time and will be made when served on the offeree (service being governed by the terms of CPR Pt 6).

The Relevant Period

This is a phrase is used in reference to the requirement to set a period of time during which the offer may be accepted without penalty.

The relevant period can be as long as the parties agree but must not be less than 21 days unless the offer is made less than 21 days before trial in which case it runs until the end of the trial.

There are restrictions on the withdrawal of offers during the relevant period, but conclusion of the period does not automatically mean the offer is withdrawn or may no longer be accepted.

However, following the 2015 revisions, part 36.9 now provides that a party can serve advance notice to withdraw its offer or amend its terms. This in essence give parties the ability to make Part 36 offers available for acceptance for a limited time only.

This allows parties to be more creative and strategic with their offers.

Offers In Soft Tissue Injury (whiplash) claims

As a result of a policy decision that pre-medical offers may encourage unmeritorious claims, CPR Pt 36.20 (6) provides that that in soft tissue injury claim, as defined by the Pre Action Protocol for Low Value

Injury claims in RTAs (see the earlier chapter on this protocol), any offer would not be effective, in the event of late acceptance or judgment, until 21 days after the defendant receives the "fixed cost medical report".

Formalities

The need to comply with the formalities of Part 36 is paramount. The new Rule addresses some of the technical point scoring that is referred to in past case law where a party to litigation claimed that a Part 36 offer did not comply with the strict wording of Part 36, for instance the case of Thewlis v Groupama [2012] EWHC 3 (TCC). Under the new CPR 36.5 (1) (b) a party only has to make it clear that the offer is "made pursuant to Part 36" (as opposed to the previous regime that demands that the offer must "state on its face that it is intended to have the consequences of Section 1 of Part 36").

The changes Part 36.5 were meant to make the formalities of a part 36 less prescriptive – so the offer only has to make it clear that the offer is "made pursuant to Part 36" rather than to state it is intended to have the consequences of Section 1 of Part 36. However case law below shows that, within the revised rules of Part 36, the form of a Part 36 offer is still as important as before.

Part 36 offers in Personal Injury Claims

Offers in personal injury claims must comply with additional requirements set out in part 36.

Claims which include a claim for future pecuniary loss are dealt with by CPR r.36.18, In such cases, parties must give consideration to whether all or part of a payment for future losses should be made by periodical payment, and in cases where periodical payments will be made must set out details of those payments, and also the lump sum element of the settlement.

In claims which include a claim for provisional damages an offer must state whether or not it includes an offer in relation to provisional damages, and if so details of the circumstances in which provisional damages will be allowed, such as the nature of the deterioration and relevant timeframes. (CPR r.36.19)

CPR r.36.22 makes provision in relation to recoverable benefits and provides that:

> *"A defendant who makes a Part 36 offer must, where relevant, state either—*
>
> *(a) "that the offer is made without regard to any liability for recoverable amounts; or*
>
> *(b) that it is intended to include any deductible amounts."*

Where the offer is intended to include any deductible amounts other provisions in the rule apply including CPR r.36.22(6) which stipulates:

"Subject to paragraph (7), the Part 36 offer must state—

> *(a) "the gross amount of compensation;*
>
> *(b) the name and amount of any deductible amounts by which the gross amount is*
>
> *reduced; and*
>
> *(c) the net amount of compensation."*

CPR r.36.22(7) confirms:

> *"If at the time the offeror makes the Part 36 offer, the offeror has applied for, but has not received, a certificate, the offeror must clarify the offer by stating the matters referred to in paragraph (6)(b) and c) not more than 7 days after receipt of the certificate."*

Identification of the net sum, one way or another, is important because CPR r.36.22(8) provides:

> *"For the purposes of rule 36.17(1)(a), a claimant fails to recover more than any sum offered (including a lump sum offered under*

rule 36.6) if the claimant fails upon judgment being entered to recover a sum, once deductible amounts identified in the judgment have been deducted, greater than the net amount stated under paragraph (6)(c)."

Defendant's offers

CPR r.36.6 confirms a Pt 36 offer by a defendant to pay a sum of money must be an offer to pay a single sum and that an offer including an offer to pay all or part of the sum at a date later than 14 days following the date of acceptance will not be treated as a Pt 36 offer unless the offeree accepts the offer. The latter provision protects, in particular, a claimant from arguments that because the offer failed to comply with the terms of CPR Pt 36 other provisions in the rule, such as the deemed costs order on acceptance, would not apply.

Improving Offers

Very often in litigation a party makes an initial offer to see if there is any appetite for settlement and then makes a further improved offer.

Under the CPR 36.9 in order to do this the following must apply:

- No notice of acceptance can have been served (CPR 36.9(1)).

- Written notice of the change of terms must be served (CPR36.9 (2)).

- The enhanced offer can be made without the permission of the court (CPR36.9 (4) (a)).

In terms of costs, the most important change is to CPR36.9 (5) which provides:

"Where the offeror changes the terms of a Part 36 offer to make it more advantageous to the offeree –

> *(a)   Such improved offer shall be treated, not as the withdrawal of the original offer; but as the making of a new Part 36 offer on the improved terms…"*

This means that you can have more than one Part 36 offer on the table at any one time, which can be used to a party's tactical advantage given the consequences which flow from the acceptances of an offer outside of the relevant period.

For example, the claimant makes a claim for breach of contract claiming £150,000. The defendant believes that the case has merit but that the damages are overstated. The defendant makes an immediate Part 36 offer at £75,000 during the pre-action correspondence which it increases to £100,000 following service of the Defence. At trial the claimant is awarded £60,000. The defendant can refer to the first offer made very early on in the process and claim enhanced costs from that date.

Withdrawing offers

It may be the case that for legal or tactical reasons a party wishes to withdraw a Part 36 offer. Again for withdrawing offers:

- Notice of Acceptance cannot have been served.

- Written notice is to be given.

- After expiry of the "relevant period" the offer can be withdrawn without permission of the court.

- The offer may be withdrawn in accordance with its terms.

CPR36.10 deals with the consequences of withdrawing the offer before the expiry of the relevant period. This means that parties can become more strategic in how they make offers by setting a date by which an offer must be accepted or the offer falls away. This can be a dangerous strategy since the traditional cost protection would similarly fall away.

However in certain cases where pressure needs to be exerted on the other party this provision may prove to be a very effective tool.

Accepting offers

CPR rr.36.11 – 36.15 deal with accepting offers.

<u>Costs consequences on acceptance</u>

The well-known costs consequences applicable on acceptance of a Pt 36 offer are set out in CPR r.36.13. There is s a deemed costs order, under CPR r.36.13(1), where an offer is accepted within the relevant period but that is subject to the exceptions found in CPR r.36.13(2) and (4) which are as follows.

- Where a defendant's Pt 36 offer relates to part only of the claim (and when serving notice of acceptance the claimant abandons the balance of the claim).

- Where a Pt 36 offer which was made less than 21 days before the start of a trial is accepted.

- Where a Pt 36 offer which relates to the whole of the claim is accepted after expiry of the relevant period.

- Where (unless it is a Pt 36 offer by the defendant relating to part only of the claim and when accepting the claimant abandons the balance of the claim) it is a Pt 36 offer which does not relate to the whole of the claim, whenever that is accepted.

Where there is a deemed costs order in favour of the claimant CPR r.36.13(3) provides that, unless fixed, those costs are to be assessed on the standard basis if not agreed. In other circumstances CPR r.36.13(4) requires the liability for costs to be determined by the court unless the parties have reached agreement.

Pre-action costs

After confirming entitlement to the "costs of the proceedings" the rule expressly adds that this includes recoverable pre-action costs but also makes express reference to CPR r.36.20 which deals with the costs consequences on acceptance of a Pt 36 offer where there are fixed costs in ex-protocol claims. There must be some concern that the express addition of the words "including their recoverable pre-action costs" may cause difficulties if a claimant accepts a pre-issue Pt 36 offer.

Before the addition of these words in the 2015 amendments to Part 36, the word "proceedings" in this context had been given a broad definition. In Solomon v Cromwell Group Plc [2011] EWCA Civ 1584; [2012] 1 W.L.R. 1048 Moore-Bick LJ held: "It is quite true that the word 'proceedings' normally refers to proceedings already pending and Part 36 as a whole is primarily directed to that situation. In that context the extension of the Rules to enable Part 36 offers to be made before proceedings have been started might be considered to be somewhat anomalous, but the terms of Part 36 as a whole make it quite clear, in my view, that steps taken in contemplation of proceedings are to be regarded as 'proceedings' for the purpose of rule 36.10(1). The effect of accepting a Part 36 offer made before a claim has been issued, therefore, is that the claimant is entitled to recover costs he has incurred in contemplation of the proceedings up to the date of acceptance insofar as they would have formed part of his recoverable costs if proceedings had already been issued."

Late acceptance

Where an offer is accepted after expiry of the relevant period CPR r.36.13(5) provides that, unless the court considers it unjust to do so, there will be an order that the claimant be awarded costs up to the expiry of the relevant period and the offeree pay the offeror's costs from that date up to the date of acceptance. CPR r.36.17(5) deals with what would be "unjust".

Claimants need to think carefully about the question of late acceptance by the defendants of Pt 36 offers. If judgment is obtained the problem will be avoided, as then the costs consequences in favour of the claimant will follow unless that be "unjust". In other circumstances the claimant may be restricted to costs on the standard basis.

Stay

CPR r.36.14 deals with other effects of acceptance of a Pt 36 offer, with the claim (or if the offer relates to part of a claim, that part) stayed on the terms of the offer.

Multiple defendants

CPR r.36.15 deals with acceptance of a Pt 36 offer made by one or more, but not all, defendants.

Costs consequences following judgment

CPR r.36.17 deals with the situation where judgment is entered and either the claimant fails to obtain a judgment more advantageous than a defendant's Pt 36 offer or judgment against the defendant is at least as advantageous to the claimant as the proposals contained in the claimant's Pt 36 offer.

The rule provides that in relation to any money claim the term "more advantageous" means better in money terms by any amount however small as does "at least as advantageous", meaning that monetary offers are to be compared strictly based on value and neither party can seek costs protection on the basis their offer was a 'near miss'. However this is subject to the provision that the offer must be a genuine attempt to settle proceedings, on which see below.

The rule provides for an "additional amount" payable to the claimant who has secured judgment at least as advantageous as their offer at, 10 per cent of damages up to a ceiling of £75,000 which was introduced as a result of the reforms following the Jackson Report, along with the other benefits of indemnity costs and enhanced interest. However, CPR r.36.17(4)(d) limits the award of the additional amount to the time when the case has been "decided". That does not appear to rule out the award of an additional amount where, for example, a judgment which is at least as advantageous to the claimant as an offer on an issue such as liability, though that will have to be held over until the case as a whole has been "decided".

Split Trials

Part 36.16 now states that after the hearing of a preliminary issue the terms of any Part 36 offer relating only to the concluded issue may be revealed to the Court.

Under CPR36.16 (3) (d) where there has been an issue based trial and there is a Part 36 offer in relation to the issues decided then that offer can be disclosed to the judge hearing the issue based trial. This means that many of the costs issues pertaining to the part 1 trial can be dealt with at that trial. However, parties will need to consider making different settlement offers and in particular structuring a Part 36 offer purely in relation to the first trial.

It should be noted that the parties cannot divulge the details of any offers that relate to the litigation in general to the judge hearing the preliminary issues but the judge "may be told whether or not there are Part 36 offers". Therefore, the judge can be made aware of the existence of an offer but not what that offer consists of. It may well be the case that if the judge becomes aware that there is a wider offer that he takes the view that the costs need to be reserved until final hearing in any event.

This provision can be used tactically by a party sub dividing their settlement offers so that certain terms are disclosed at an earlier stage if appropriate.

Cynical Offers

Parties will sometimes make offers which are set at such a level that they would never be accepted by the other side. This issue had attracted a lot of case law in the past, with parties claiming that the automatic consequences of Part 36 should not flow in circumstances where they could never be expected to accept the offer made.

The changes made to Part 36.17 are an attempt to address this with Part 36.17(4)(b) now allowing a Court to take into consideration whether an offer was a genuine attempt to settle the proceedings when considering whether to apply the automatic consequences of Part 36.

Cost Budgets

The general rule when a party fails to file a cost budget is that its recovery of costs is limited to Court fees only.

Part 36.23 now provides that when it comes to applying the automatic cost consequences of Part 36 to a party who failed to file a cost budget that party's recoverability will be limited to 50% of the costs otherwise recoverable and not just limited to Court fees. So, if a party fails to file a cost budget in time, the new provisions under Part 36.23 provides a means of making a more substantial recovery of costs than would otherwise be possible.

The intention is that the other party to litigation does not have carte blanche to turn down reasonable offers and run the litigation in an unreasonable way safe believing that even in the event of a bad result they only have to pay court fees.

Pre-Issue Offers

We need to look at are the changes made to parts 36.7 and 36.13 in respect of offers made pre-issue. Under the previous regime the there used to be some uncertainty in respect of the cost consequences of pre-issues offers which were accepted before the commencement of proceedings.

This was because the old part 36.10 provided that the claimant would be entitled to the **costs of the proceedings** up to the date on which the offer was accepted. The changes to part 36.7 and 36.13 seek to clarify this position providing that an offer can be made pre-issue and that a claimant's automatic entitlement to reasonably incurred costs includes their recoverable pre-action costs. There is still a little uncertainty in this area as what is not clear is whether a recovering party will need to commence cost only proceedings in order to recover these costs.

Appeals

CPR r.36.4 deals expressly with appeals and provides:

"(1) Except where a Part 36 offer is made in appeal proceedings, it shall have the consequences set out in this Section only in relation to the costs of the proceedings in respect of which it is made, and not in relation to the costs of any appeal from a decision in those proceedings."

Paragraph 2 then goes on to specify the manner in which definitions and terminology relevant to appeals apply in place of those relating to claims at first instance.

The result in an extension of Part 36 to apply to appeals. In the event of an appeal the parties will need to consider repeating (or renewing as varied) offers made in the proceedings under appeal as well as offers made specifically for the purposes of the appeal.

Detailed Assessment

CPR r.47.20, although not expressly referred to in CPR Pt 36, adopts the Pt 36 procedure, including costs consequences, for offers to settle in detailed assessment proceedings. The absence of reference to CPR Pt 47 in CPR Pt 36 suggests these are to operate as separate regimes, hence costs will not be regarded as an issue preventing the case being "decided" nor should Pt 36 benefits in the substantive claim prevent these being awarded, where appropriate, in subsequent costs proceedings.

Clarification

CPR r.36.8 deals with clarification of Pt 36 offers. If a request for clarification is refused, it is open to a party to apply for an Order for clarification.

Requested for clarification may be used in arrange of ways, including

- Clarification of the terms of an offer, where these appear ambiguous

- Requesting information in relation to the basis of an offer (such as a breakdown fo figures)

- Testing whether an offer complies with Part 36.

There is little guidance on the circumstances in which a request for clarification is justified under the rule, or when a court will grant an order, though it is likely orders will be rare, given that the courts wish to deter satellite litigation.

Requests for clarification may nonetheless provide valuable additional information in relation to an offer, where the offeror is prepared to provide that information. Where the offeror refuses a request, the failure may be used in relation to subsequent disputes on costs (where automatic consequences of Part 36 do not apply) for example on the basis the offer failed to engage in the offered efforts to resolve the dispute by exploring the offer or, in some cases, by demonstrating the offer was not compliant with Part 36 (see the case of Patience v Tanner, below)

Recent Case Law

Jockey Club Racecourse Ltd v Willmott Dixon Construction Ltd

This case relates the changes to Part 36.17 with the Court now being required to take into consideration whether an offer was a genuine attempt to settle the litigation when considering the automatic consequences of Part 36.

In this case the claimant brought proceedings against the defendant in respect of the design and construction of a new grandstand at Epsom Race Course. Directions were given for a split trial on liability. The Claimant made a Part 36 offer to accept liability for 95% of the damages to be assessed.

The Defendant did not accept this offer in the relevant period but just before the Pre-Trial Review the Defendant conceded liability.

The claimant applied for indemnity costs on the defendant's failure to accept its Part 36 offer.

The defendant argued that this was not a genuine Part 36 offer either because it did not reflect an available outcome at trial, or because it came close to requiring total capitulation by the defendant.

The judge noted that as this was a claim where the outcome could only be success or failure for either party, and there was not room for apportionment of liability, a 95% liability was not an available outcome at trial. However he held that this not mean that an offer of settlement for 95% was not a valid Part 36 offer stating that whilst it was hardly gen-erous it could not be described "all take and no give".

The judge awarded the claimant indemnity costs from a date four months after the offer rather than at the end of the relevant period.

This case shows that following the changes the Court will view each case on its own facts and parties should not be afraid to high offer provided this fits with the context of the wider litigation.

Sugar Hut Group Ltd & Others v AJ Insurance

This is a Court of Appeal case in which it overturned a first instance decision which had ordered the Claimant to pay the Defendant's costs for the period following the Defendant's Part 36 offer, even though the claimant had beaten the offer by about 10%.

The first instance judge had found that, even though the defendant's offer had been made on a global basis, the claimants had been unreas-onable in continuing to pursue certain heads of loss when they ultimately had recovered less than the value attributed to that element of the claim in the defendant's offer.

In this case the first instance judge had effectively penalised the claimants by treating the offer as if it contained separate offers rather than it being one single indivisible offer. The Court of Appeal allowed the appeal concluding that the judge had been mistaken treating the Part 36 offers as containing provision to settle a specific head of claim for a certain sum when the offer had not been made on that basis. It also confirmed that the claimant had beaten the defendant's offer by a considerable sum and pointed out that there was no longer a "near miss rule" which means there was no reason to deprive the claimants of their costs following the offer.

Hertel v Saunders

This case highlights the need to comply with requirements of Part 36 in order to ensure that an offer attracts the benefits of Part 36.

The claimant brought proceedings against the defendants seeking a declaration that there was a partnership or joint venture between the two, together with other relief. The defendants denied there was any form of partnership or joint venture between the two.

The claimants later served a draft amended claim form and particulars of claim which put forward an alternative position that there had been an agreement between the two companies under which certain sums were due.

The defendants put forward a put forward a purported Part 36 offer which was said to be

> *"an offer in settlement of the claimants' proposed claim, by amendment for an account based on an agreement".*

This offer was accepted by the claimants who confirmed they would abandon the rest of their claim. On accepting the offer the claimants sought an order for their costs under Part 36.10(2). But the Court held that the defendants offer was not a valid part 36 offer as the proposed claim was not part of the claim when the offer was made an so the offer did not meet the requirements of CPR 36.5(1) being that the offer must *"state whether it relates to the whole of the claim or to part of it or to an issue which arises in it and if so which part or issue".*

This case is interesting as while the changes to Part 36 were aimed at avoiding excess technicality in the interpretation of the rules this case illustrates that some of the requirements of Part 36 may still be open to a highly technical interpretation. It also is contradictory to the fact that now a Part 36 offer can be made before proceedings are issued that this case suggests one cannot be made in respect of a claim that is proposed but not yet brought.

Caselaw on formal requirements of a part 36 offer

We have noted above that the latest revisions to Part 36 reduce the formal requirements. However there remain rules in relation to mandatory information, which must be satisfied in order to make a valid Part 36 offer. Further, practitioners still often have to consider offers made before the revisions to Part 36

There are a line of cases all stressing the need for compliance with the rules on form and content when making Pt 36 offers. Whilst the Court of Appeal judgment in C v D appeared to suggest a more relaxed approach to form and content so, perhaps, a mere reference to "Pt 36" might suffice to make the offer effective, that overlooks the emphasis placed in the very case on the need for compliance with the rules on form and content. The pitfalls were highlighted by the judgment in Thewlis v Groupama Insurance Co Ltd which at first sight seemed almost indistinguishable from C v D but which had some important differences of real significance to the validity of the offer for the purposes of Pt 36. Whilst the decision in Thewlis has been the subject of criticism the judgment in that case it has since been roundly supported by the Court of Appeal in Shaw v Merthyr Tydfil CBC.8 That judgment in Shaw reflects the very strict approach to the rules on form and content taken under the pre-April 2015 version of CPR Pt 36, in particular the need for an offeror to comply precisely with the terms of the former CPR r.36.2(2).

Prior to the issue of proceedings the claimant made a Pt 36 offer. That letter was headed "Pt 36 Offer" and read: "Our client offers to accept the sum of £2,000 in full and final settlement of the claim for general and special damages, such sums to be inclusive of interest together with payment [of] her reasonable costs to be detailed assessed in default of agreement. This offer remains open for a period of 21 days from the date of receipt of the offer, after which time the offer may only be accepted if the parties agree their liability in respect of costs or the court provides its permission for late acceptance."

The claim was, though only following an appeal, successful with damages of £6,510 being awarded. When costs were being assessed the claimant contended she was entitled to the benefits conferred by CPR r.36.14, having beaten her own offer, including indemnity costs. The district judge assessing costs held that the claimant's offer was not a valid Pt 36 offer, following Thewlis. Accordingly, costs were assessed on the standard basis. The claimant appealed this ruling, but that appeal was dismissed by the Court of Appeal.

After observing that CPR Pt 36 provides for certain costs consequences Maurice Kay LJ went on to hold:

> *"However, all this is predicated upon the offer having been compliant with the requirements of Part 36. Rule 36.2(2) is expressed in mandatory language and its requirements have been held to be mandatory—see PHI Group Ltd v Robert West Consulting Ltd [2012] EWCA Civ 588, especially at*
>
> *paragraph 25, per Lloyd LJ. Five mandatory requirements are set out including (b) that the offer states on its face that it is intended to have the consequences of section 1 of Part 36."*

In this case the offer failed to expressly state that it was "intended to have the consequences" of CPR Pt 36. Furthermore, the offer did not identify a relevant period but, rather, was made in terms reflecting the language of the rule before amended with effect from April 6, 2007. Accordingly, Maurice Kay LJ held: "In these circumstances, as a matter of form, the offer did not satisfy the mandatory requirements of Part

36. Accordingly it was not a Part 36 offer, even though the letter described it as one. This case is indistinguishable from Thewlis which the judge followed with manifest reluctance."

It was in these circumstances that the Court of Appeal went on to reject criticism there had been of the judgment in Thewlis.

Patience v Tanner and Burrell v Clifford

A couple more cases which highlight the need to conform with the Part 36 regime are **Patience v Tanner** and **Burrell v Clifford**

In Patience v Tanner the defendant made an offer to settle the claimant's claim for specific performance. The offer was open for acceptance for 21 days only, after which it would lapse. It also said nothing in respect of the cost consequences of accepting the offer. The claimant queried the position on costs but the defendant did not respond.

About a week before trial the defendant repeated the terms of its offer and the claimant accepted the offer.

At first instance the judge recognised the offer was not compliant with Part 36 but nonetheless ordered that the defendant was to bear the claimant's costs up to the end of relevant period in respect of the defendant's first offer and the claimant was to bear the defendant's costs thereafter.

The claimant appealed this decision and the Court of Appeal allowed the appeal in part highlighting the flaws in the defendant's offer including the fact that the first offer made no reference to costs. The Court of Appeal therefore substituted its own view which was that the claimant was entitled to costs up to the end of the relevant period of the first offer and that after this date each party was to bear its own costs.

In Burrell v Clifford the claimant was awarded damages of £5,000 in a privacy claim against the defendant. Despite the fact the claimant had succeeded in its claim, the defendant argued that the claimant should be ordered to pay some of its costs as the claimant had failed to beat the defendant's offer of £5,000 damaged plus reasonable costs of up to £5,000 (inclusive of VAT) made on a "without prejudice save as to costs" basis.

The Court held that the claimant was entitled to reasonable costs in spite of the offer as at the time the offer was made the claimant's costs were well in excess of £5,000, which meant the offer was inadequate.

The judge stated that in order to obtain the cost protection the defendant should have offered to pay the claimants reasonable costs to be assessed – as would have been the case if the offer had been made under part 36.

While the changes to the rules were meant to simplify the part 36 regime, these cases highlight that when it comes to part 36 each case will turn on its own facts and the only sure way to obtain the costs advantages of part 36 is to make an offer in strict compliance with it provisions and leave that offer on the table until judgement is given.

<u>Detailed assessment</u>

Two recent cases have considered the operation of CPR Pt 36 in the context of detailed assessment. In Cashman v Mid Essex Hospital Services NHS Trust the claimant's claim against the defendant was settled on terms that the defendant would pay £90,000 damages together with costs to be assessed on the standard basis if not agreed. The claimant served a bill of costs for about £262,000. About seven months before the detailed assessment hearing the claimant made a Pt 36 offer, in the costs proceedings, of £152,500. Costs were assessed at £173,693.78 at the detailed assessment.

That judgment was "more advantageous" to the claimant than the proposal contained in the claimant's Pt 36 offer on costs. Accordingly, under the terms of CPR r.47.20, the provisions of CPR r.36.14(3) applied, unless that would be unjust. The Master held that it would not be unjust for the consequences provided for under CPR r.36.14(3) to apply, save for the additional amount. The Master concluded that it would be unjust to order the defendant to pay the claimant the prescribed additional amount, at 10 per cent of the costs as assessed, explaining:

"Had the rule permitted me to allow a figure fixed by applying the prescribed percentage to the difference between the sum which the claimant offered to accept and the sum which was allowed, then I think that may have been a just result, but that is not what the rule anticipates. In circumstances where there has been a significant reduction in the claimant's bill, it seems to me that it would be unjust to reward the claimant with an additional amount prescribed by 36.14(3)(d)."

The claimant appealed. Giving judgment in the appeal Slade J concluded this was a case where the Master had fallen into the temptation referred to by Sir David Eady in Downing v Peterborough & Stamford Hospitals NHS Foundation Trust when he said:

"It is elementary that a judge who is asked to depart from the norm, on the ground that it would be 'unjust' not to do so, should not be tempted to make an exception merely because he or she thinks the regime itself harsh or unjust. There must be something about the particular circumstances of the case which takes it out of the norm." Moreover, Slade J held: "The approach adopted by the Master penalises the Claimant for making what turned out to be a reasonable Part 36 offer. It is the terms of the Part 36 offer not the level of the sums claimed in the bill of costs which are to be considered under CPR 36.14(4). Whilst all the relevant circumstances are to be considered in deciding whether it would be unjust to make an award under any of the paragraphs of CPR 36.14(3), it was not suggested that there was any particular feature or consequence of the bill of costs other than its size which would render the making of an order under CPR 36.14(3)(d) unjust.

There being no reason advanced by the defendant, other than the high level of the bill of costs, why it would be unjust for there to be an order for an additional amount under CPR r.36.14(3)(d) Slade J ruled: "In those circumstances, properly directing himself, in my judgment the Master could only have concluded that it was not unjust to make an order under CPR 36.14(3)(d). Accordingly this court orders that the Claimant is entitled to an additional award calculated in accordance with that subparagraph." In Shepherd v Hughes 11 the issue for the court was whether, following provisional assessment but prior to any detailed assessment, the offeree was at liberty to accept a Pt 36 offer on costs made prior to the provisional assessment, that offer being more advantageous to the offeree than the outcome of the provisional assessment.

A Pt 36 offer, which has not been withdrawn, can generally be accepted at any time but the terms of CPR r.36.9(3), as the rule read prior to April 2013, required the offeree to obtain permission from the court to accept an offer once "the trial has started". As HHJ Seys-Llewellyn QC observed, the key issue was whether "… the detailed assessment hearing has started, by reason that there was a provisional assessment or not?" The judge concluded the answer was to be found within the terms of CPR r.47.15 and found:

"Thus, all of those provisions are subject to the introduction that this Rule, 47.15, ' applies to any detailed assessment proceedings ' (my emphasis). Thus, it seems, that enables and informs me to construe the reference in CPR 36.9(3) to a detailed assessment hearing as including the provisional assessment which is intrinsically a part of the structure which may lead to a detailed assessment hearing; and thus requiring that the court's permission is required to accept a part [36] offer where the provisional assessment has been made."

<u>General provisions</u>

General provisions relating to acceptance of Pt 36 offers are now set out in CPR r.36.11. This makes no changes of note to the existing version of the rule.

<u>Split-trial cases</u>

CPR r.36.12 does, however, deal expressly with the potential problem of Pt 36 offers made in cases where there is a split trial. Sensibly, to avoid arguments about whether an offer survives such a trial, the new rule makes express provision to deal with this situation.

If an offer relates only to parts of the claim or issues already decided such an offer can no longer be accepted after trial of a preliminary issue. Any other Pt 36 offers cannot be accepted earlier than seven clear days after judgment is given or handed down in such a trial, which affords the offeror a window to withdraw or change the offer which seems only appropriate given that the determination of the preliminary point may have a bearing on the appropriate terms for settlement of the remaining issues.

Summary

- Part 36 offers are not the only form of offer which may be made in the course of proceedings or taken into account by the Court on the matter of costs.

- However, offers which comply with part 36 generally carry automatic costs consequences, increasing predictability and allowing parties to make strong offers which incentivise their opponents to settle

- In order to amount to a Part 36 offer, an offer letter must comply with relevant formal requirements.

- Part 36 can be used effectively in split trials by making separate offers.

- Part 36 can be used in costs proceedings.

CHAPTER EIGHT
MEDIATION

Types of Mediation

There are essentially two types of mediation; facilitative and evaluative. Facilitative mediation is by far the most common model used in England and Wales. Evaluative mediation is rather different. Although the lines of distinction between the two may appear to blur, in reality the difference between them is profound.

Evaluative Mediation

In evaluative mediation at some point the mediator will express a view (probably simultaneously to all parties) on the strengths and weaknesses of their respective cases. He or she might indicate which arguments might succeed and which might fail. The mediator might even express a view on what might constitute a fair and reasonable settlement. This will not happen in facilitative mediation. In our view, evaluative mediation is most appropriate in personal injury claims and it is best if the mediator has some experience in dealing with personal injury claims, much as a family mediator is often someone who is a family practitioner. Otherwise, the mediator will not understand the issues, particularly as to quantum.

Facilitative mediation

In facilitative mediation a neutral third party, the mediator, assists the parties to settle their disputes. The mediator is the catalyst. The presence of an independent third party is the key distinguishing feature of the process. Facilitative mediation is a process of managed negotiation.

There is no doubt that mediation is an extremely effective way to settle disputes. Evidence from solicitors, barristers, mediators, and mediation service providers broadly confirms that between 75% and 80% of disputes which are referred to mediation settle either on the day or very shortly thereafter.

The Mediator

Mediators all work in different ways, partly through their character and partly through their training and expertise. Certainly there is no set formula but there are certain common threads. The mediator must be entirely neutral and independent. The mediator brings a fresh and trusted mind to what is often an old problem. Trust and integrity are key watch-words. Their role is to aid communication between the parties, to assist them to overcome emotional blockages, to focus their attention and effort on the problems and moreover their solutions. They can help each side to understand the other side's case or even their own case (and its weaknesses, which they and sometimes their advisors have been unable or unwilling to look at). Mediators can suggest new avenues to explore, to identify and work to overcome deadlock, to unlock and release any of the entrenched positions and in some cases the ill feeling that can accumulate in the course of a dispute.

The mediator has control over the process but not over the resolution of the dispute. So they can decide who should take part in joint meetings, who should take part in private meetings (just solicitors or just the parties or just the experts). They can require the parties to prepare summaries of their best points or schedules of claims.

They cannot make any orders as such. A mediator unlike an arbitrator cannot order the production of documents. So if there are crucial documents that you must have in handling a dispute, do not go to a mediation until you have got them. Whether documents ever are crucial of course is a matter of judgment.

Against this background, perhaps it is obvious that the mediator has no power to make a final determination of issues between the parties. They will not issue an Award or the equivalent of a judgment; nor will they express any view on the merits of each party's case (cf: evaluative mediation). Either the parties reach a settlement between them or the mediation will break up without a resolution. The parties will be left

either to pursue formal legal process, perhaps to negotiate or to reconvene a mediation on a later day.

Key features of mediation

Voluntary nature

Mediation is voluntary. In Court process the Court can "encourage" the
parties to refer their dispute to mediation with the threat of costs penalties. This does not apply with arbitration.

Since the whole process is voluntary parties can walk out of mediation
whenever they wish and, although it is rare, sometimes they do just
that. This would be unthinkable in arbitration.

Without prejudice

Mediation is without prejudice. Anything created solely for the purpose
of the mediation and anything said on the day is without prejudice. In
the event that no settlement is reached neither party can rely on any
documents created for the mediation nor on anything said on the day in
the course of the formal mediation.

Confidentiality

Mediation is private and confidential. Nothing which is said in the
course of the mediation can be discussed outside the mediation nor
revealed to any third party. This stipulation of confidentiality is generally embodied in the Mediation Agreement which is signed (usually on
the day) to regulate the mediation process.

However, once something is said or revealed it cannot be unsaid. If a
case does not settle anything which is revealed at the mediation even if
it cannot be used in the litigation process might then influence the conduct of that litigation. As a matter of strict proof or evidence, parties
may be then alerted to things they did not previously know. They may
be prompted to hunt down alternative sources of evidence to assist

them in proving their case later at a final hearing. This is one illustration of the care that is needed in participating in mediation. Mediation is not merely a matter of common sense. It is a skill.

Costs of mediation

Unless otherwise agreed it is important to note that the mediator's fees and expenses are shared equally between the parties and both parties bear these costs.

The Mediation Process

When to mediate

Some say the proper approach to any dispute is to negotiate, if that fails mediate and if that fails arbitrate (or litigate). That may be an ideal but is not always appropriate.

As a generalisation mediation should only be used when the case is ready; that is when both or all sides to the dispute recognise that they have an incentive to settle. When this should be is a matter of fine judgment and will differ from case to case. In this respect every case is unique.

- Should it be after exchange of letters before action, when an outline of the claim is set out?

- Should it be after an exchange of pleadings, when the issues have been narrowed?

- Should it be after disclosure of documents when the evidence to evaluate those pleadings has been disclosed?

- Should it be after exchange of witness statements when the evidence on both sides should be that much clearer?

- Should it be finally after exchange of experts' reports?

If there is to be a saving in cost, and if the many other benefits of mediation are to be accessed, it is wise to engage in mediation at the earliest possible stage.

Selecting a Mediator

When selecting a mediator, the usual process involves contacting a mediation provider and obtaining details of three available mediators and the parties then select one. Usually the parties also take soundings as to the experience of using the mediators concerned. It is necessary to establish what the mediator's fees will be and payment is made before the mediation takes place. Parties normally bear the costs of the mediation themselves and it is not recoverable from the other party as costs of the litigation although it is included in costs budgets as an expense.

Selecting a mediation format

Mediation can involve a full day or be time limited. Telephone and online mediation can be equally as effective as a physical meeting and be particularly appropriate in personal injury claims where a party is unable to attend a physical meeting.

Preparing for the mediation

The parties normally exchange position statements in advance of the mediation and send a bundle of key documents to the mediator so that he or she can prepare. Where the parties respective positions are set out in existing documents (as when there is a detailed schedule and counter schedule) these may take the place of the position statement.

Parties will be provided with a copy of the mediation agreement by the mediator, for signature. While signing may take place on the day of the mediation, parties should review the agreement well in advance to allow any queries to be clarified. The agreement will include terms in relation to the mediators' fees, confidentiality, the mediator's powers, limitations of liability and procedure. In relation to the procedure, the agreement will often include or be accompanied by a document which sets this out, or it may simply confirm the mediators' powers in relation to process.

Outline of the mediation

At a typical mediation, there is normally a joint opening session and then the mediator shuttles between the parties separately to negotiate. Although the legal arguments are important, the negotiations often come down to a discussion of figures that would be satisfactory in terms of settlement. At the end of the process, assuming that settlement is reached, the parties or the mediator draw up a settlement agreement or consent order for filing at Court.

The opening session

Usually the mediation opens with a joint meeting attended by the mediator and all the parties. When that joint meeting is concluded, the parties break up into separate private rooms and the mediator effectively conducts shuttle diplomacy between them.

Anything which is said at the joint session is confidential

The private sessions

The private sessions are an opportunity for the mediator to work with individual parties to explore their case, and the other party's position (so far as this has been conveyed prior to the mediation, or by the mediator with authority of the party involved) in order to assist them in analyzing strengths and weaknesses, and to move towards resolution of the claim.

Anything which is discussed in the private sessions is confidential and cannot be revealed by the mediator to the other party or parties unless and until they are specifically authorised by the revealing party to do so. This is one of the most unusual and effective features of the process. By contrast, would you reveal to a judge or arbitrator your weaknesses or details of any commercial or financial pressures you face? Obviously not. Under this cloak of confidentiality the parties often reveal to mediators the most extraordinary things, which the mediators can then use (with their authority) to fashion a bargain between the parties.

Subsequent joint sessions

The mediator may consider that it will be beneficial to hold a further joint session or sessions as a mediation progresses. This will very much depend upon the mediator's preferred way of working. The mediator may do so in order to convey a view (on process or, in evaluative mediation, on the case) to the parties together. As with the initial joint session, neither party is obliged to provide any information to the other, and the session is confidential and without prejudice to the claim.

Benefits of Mediation

In some respects it is an astonishingly effective process for the following main reasons.

Independent third party

First, it involves an independent third party. Mediation has its roots in international diplomacy and this can be seen in how the mediator after the usual opening session when all the parties are together operates as a trusted diplomat shuttling between two or more sides and drawing together the threads of the deal. The parties are encouraged by mediators to look at their interests and needs, instead of their rights and wants (as they might perceive them) and most particularly to focus on the alternative if a dispute is not settled. It is often far easier for a third party to do this than it is to hear this message from one's own advisor or indeed from one's opponent.

Decision makers

Secondly, mediation involves decision makers, rather than just lawyers. It is essential that a person with full authority to settle the dispute attends on the day. Strictly speaking full authority means the authority to settle anywhere on the full spectrum from 0% to 100%. It is understood that those who attend often do not have wholly unlimited authority but generally they do have authority to make any deal within sensible parameters. The fact that they are there or available on the telephone, in the case of insurers, and participating in the process is crucial.

Timetable, structure, dynamic

Thirdly, the timetable, the structure and the dynamic of the process. Mediation can focus minds on resolving the dispute. Many people say if parties can negotiate to settle their disputes they should do so and isn't mediation after all just a process of managed negotiation? Absolutely; but often parties cannot negotiate for one reason or another. Some lawyers are highly skilled in identifying risk in litigation at an early stage and seeking resolution by negotiation, but to strike a deal all parties must engage in negotiation and shrug off personal struggles and even vendettas.

By contrast, negotiations can drag. They have no timetable (other than the cold chill of an approaching hearing or a deadline to produce documents or statements). There might be multiple parties involved and negotiations can break down at the whim of one. When all attend a mediation, prepare for it in advance in accordance with a set timetable and then participate actively on the day, all are drawn in.

Shared sense of purpose

It is accepted that some parties go into mediation with absolutely no intention of settling. Their only purpose in attending (if they have not been compelled by a Court to do so) is to find out as much as they can about the other side's case while giving away as little as possible about their own. But these are the minority. Most cases reach a point where all parties want to settle and facilitative mediation makes best use of that shared sense of purpose.

Unusual deals

Through mediation disputes can be resolved by deals which go way beyond any kind of apportionment of the issues between the parties or any sort of adjudication of who is right and who is wrong.

There might be a dispute over an insurance policy; are the insurers compelled to pay or not? If that was referred to a Court or an arbitration tribunal there would be findings of fact and conclusions of law. Is the policy binding? Are the Underwriters entitled to avoid it? Is there a breach of warranty, does the policy cover the circumstances of loss? If it goes to a hearing both will take the risk of losing. However through a mediation they might negotiate the settlement of that claim.

Substitute day in court

Another factor is that mediation is a substitute for a day in Court, without the risk and cost of a trial. The parties can say exactly what they think about the other side directly to the other side. That is never going to happen in Court nor in an arbitration tribunal where there is a fine structure for the running of the case. The parties have an opportunity to vent their feelings, again without the risk or the cost of going to a final hearing. This can be cathartic; it can release pent up tension that would otherwise preclude negotiation.

Relationship and reputation

Mediation minimises the risk of damage to relationships and to reputations. Instead of being evermore deeply entrenched in an adversarial process the senior parties, the decision makers, can be engaged in constructive discussion with their counterparts in a manner that simply cannot and will not be achieved through traditional dispute handling. Their relationship may even be enhanced. In a clinical negligence case, obtaining an apology or explanation may be important, as well as learning lessons for the future.

As to reputations individuals can adopt a particular stance in handling a particular problem and chosen to stick by that stance even when evidence emerges to suggest that it is unwise. The ultimate damage to reputation is to those who feel then compelled to go into the witness box to give evidence only to find that their evidence has been treated as unsatisfactory by a tribunal.

When mediation may not be appropriate

There are some key things that mediation cannot achieve. Mediation cannot generally interrupt a time bar. However, in consumer cases, the limitation period is extended to 8 weeks after the conclusion of the ADR Process, under a new S.33B of the Limitation Act 1980. We would certainly suggest that such an extension is applied to personal injury claims. Of course, the parties can agree a limitation standstill agreement between them, to extend limitation to take part in ADR, so saving the costs of issuing proceedings for limitation purposes. So there is no point embarking on the process of the preparation for and attendance at a mediation without ensuring that a time bar has been protected.

In what other circumstances should mediation not be used? Obviously because of its essentially private nature there is no point is using mediation if one of the key objectives in any dispute is to obtain a precedent. But this is not a consideration in a dispute which is subject to a binding arbitration agreement. Arbitration Awards, in the absence of an appeal, are private and are not the vehicle by which precedents are created. In cases where fraud is an issue, mediation is unlikely to be appropriate, although it may save costs of proving the fraud.

There is no purpose in using mediation to resolve a dispute if a key objective is publicity. The whole mediation process is wrapped in a blanket of confidentiality and any final resolution, in the form of a signed settlement agreement, will never see the light of day. Most Mediation Agreements require there to be an agreement in writing for a settlement to be concluded. Those settlement agreements are subject to the same duties of confidentiality which apply to the rest of the mediation process.

Critical Factors for Success in Personal Injury/Clinical Negligence Mediations

There are a number of factors which are critical to the successful mediation of personal injury and clinical negligence claims. These range from how and in what circumstances the mediation is set up, to the personality and skill-set of the mediator involved to the "buy-in" from the solicitors and litigants involved.

- First and foremost it is important that the parties mediate at the right time to maximise the chances of the matter settling (and if not settle then to substantially narrow the issues between the parties). This may vary from case to case but clearly the mediation must take place when both parties are in receipt of sufficient information on liability, causation and quantum to allow them to make a proper evaluation of the case. This could be towards the end of the protocol, pre-action process, before proceedings have been issued and crucially before the costs substantially increase (especially following the recent court fee hike). This ensures that litigation is dealt with in the most cost effective way.

- The parties then need to decide on the appropriate type of mediation. Should it be a telephone mediation? Should the mediation be time-limited? A good mediator can guide the parties through the options ensuring that the type of mediation selected is appropriate for the parties and is geared towards settlement.

- There needs to be full engagement from the outset from the mediator and the parties. This involves pro-active input by the mediator making initial contact with the parties and setting out clear parameters as to how the mediation will proceed. Early engagement means that the parties can agree on the content of the agreed bundle and the format of the position papers. It is important that the content is controlled so that the mediation is focused. Further it should not be a full bundle of all papers where there would be a real risk of the mediation becoming a "mini trial". Further a good mediator will scope out the relevant issues on the telephone in advance of the mediation so that when the parties do meet at mediation they are focused on the issues thus ensuring that settlement is more likely. It is also important that the parties come armed with information in relation to costs so that all matters can be wrapped up.

• Although perhaps sometimes dismissed as administration, the venue for the mediation is an important consideration. Both parties need to feel comfortable in their surroundings. We ensure that both parties have proper facilities including a fully equipped room for their private discussions. Further the venue needs to be arranged in conjunction with the parties so that neither party feels as if they are being disadvantaged in terms of travel.

• It is critically important that there is empathy between the mediator and the parties. Litigation is a combative process culminating in trial where each side will have its witnesses cross examined with each side trying to discredit the other's witnesses. Mediation, by contrast, allows the parties to look at the issues in a more constructive, balanced way without any judgment calls being made as to a witness's credibility. Further, if the mediator can allow the claimant to feel heard, making them realise that they understand what they believe that they have suffered and give them an opportunity to express their emotions without feeling inhibited, this can assist in bringing the parties together and facilitate settlement. By taking a non-combative approach a mediator is better able to deliver bad news in an understanding, sympathetic way. By utilising this approach and taking the heat out of the situation, a good mediator can assist in situations where, by way of example, a claimant does not have realistic prospects of success and needs to be guided towards discontinuing a claim.

- The mediator's style at mediation is important. In personal injury and clinical negligence claims, the best way to open matters up and to start proper dialogue is to actively encourage the claimant to set out his or her concerns so that they feel properly engaged in the process. A good mediator will be able to gauge whether the claim is more likely to settle as a result of joint sessions or whether "shuttle diplomacy" is likely to get better results. It is not a one size fits all. A good mediator will recognise this and manage matters accordingly.

- Adopting an interventionist approach at the mediation leads to more cases being settled. In addition, this style of mediation leaves the parties feeling that they have been heard and actively engaged in the process.

- It is also extremely important that those who can give authority to settle are in attendance or easily contactable so that a settlement can be finalised.

- If the matter is settled on the day then the mediator should assist the parties in drawing up the terms of agreement so that the possibility of there being any further dispute on the terms can be minimised.

- Sometimes matters are not settled on the day and parties need to go away from the mediation and reflect on what has been said. Very often there is a further window of opportunity for cases to settle in the days following the mediation. The mediator should follow matters up by telephone to see if the parties require our further involvement to try and resolve matters.

- It is important to remember that mediation is a flexible tool and sometimes what is required to settle a case is not a remedy

which a party could obtain at trial. A good mediator will have
that in mind when dealing with a case and exploring the options
available with the parties.

Prepare pre mediation

If you are attending a mediation, it is advisable to bear in mind the following:-

- Choose a mediator and type of mediation (online, telephone or
  in person)

- Prepare the client

- Explain the process

- Explain the mediator's role

- Agree on mediation strategy

- Be aware of best case and worst case outcomes and strengths and
  weaknesses of both sides' cases

- Analyse the negotiation style and objectives of the opposing
  decision maker

- Decide on offers and parameters of settlement

- Consider costs incurred to date and costs to be incurred. Can
  any deal be done?

- Prepare case summary

- Obtain up to date costs information so that the issue of costs can be dealt with as well as the underlying claim"

At the Mediation

If you are attending a mediation, we have some top tips to bear in mind:-

- Use the opening joint session to your advantage

- Open your negotiations positively

- Set the atmosphere for the negotiations

- Get to know the other party and establish a rapport

- Speak calmly and don't insult the other party

- Do not fear expressing emotion

- Put out the first two or three negotiating points that the other decision maker is to think about

- Do not repeat the Case summary

- Actively Listen

- Explain when you will need to leave.

- Use the Separate exploratory sessions to your advantage

- In the first meeting with the mediator review the opening session and start creating a working relationship with the mediator.

- Ask for and give information to enable you and the other party to understand.

- Present the legal issues clearly and decisively.

- Challenge precisely any errors and differing perceptions if it is essential to do so in your negotiating strategy.

- Use the bargaining and decision making phase decisively

- Enter the negotiation and decision phase as soon as your strategy allows. Do not avoid decision making.

- Do not be afraid of deadlock and use the mediator to break deadlock

- Thoroughly review and understand the style of negotiation and positions used

- Try to use principled negotiation in the final phase

- Don't give up

- Concentrate on the figures but don't forget the personal element

- Don't blackmail but do offer carrots

- Consider whether to bluff or double bluff.

- Consider how to break a deadlock by issuing an ultimatum but be prepared to have bluff called.

- Consider whether to reveal any persuasive information other party is not privy to or to keep back for litigation.

- Leave enough time to draw up a settlement agreement

- Consider whether to have a final meeting with the other party.

After the Mediation

- File any Consent or Tomlin Order at Court if there are live proceedings.

- If the case did not settle, review the file and offers made during the mediation and consider making a Part 36 or other offer to resolve the matter.

Summary

- There are several different approaches to mediation or styles of mediation.

- Mediation uses a third party independent mediator to negotiate between the parties.

- It is voluntary and without prejudice.

- The parties bear the costs of the mediation equally and it is not recoverable unless otherwise agreed.

- Mediation is particularly suitable in personal injury claims because there is often a large amount of emotion involved as well as the legal issues.

- Mediation is best used as early as possible in the process to maximise costs savings but not before the parties have sufficient information, such as expert reports.

CHAPTER NINE
JOINT SETTLEMENT
MEETINGS

Given they are one of the most frequently employed methods of ADR in larger personal injury claims, it may be surprising that there are few rules and little guidance in relation to joint Settlement Meeting ("JSM") or the steps leading up to one.

In this chapter, we set out to explain the considerations which go to understanding when a JSM is likely to assist in a claim and how to go about preparing for one. As it is the model most commonly employed at present, we will discuss face to face JSMs for much of the chapter. However, we will conclude by considering alternative models such as a telephone "JSM", which may be proportionate to lower value cases, and the opportunities offered by technology.

The Objective of a JSM

In many cases a JSM will, as the name suggests, be organised with a view to settlement of the whole claim. However, this is not always the case, and it is worth considering at the outset the other objectives which might be pursued.

JSMs in relation to an issue

It is possible to have a JSM to discuss a single issue or group of issues in relation to a claim, though it will always be important to consider whether the saving achieved by resolving that issue will outweigh the costs that would be incurred in the alternative.

For example, a JSM may be justified in relation to liability alone, particularly where there is a significant amount of evidence to be considered and/or issues of contributory negligence or joint liability which can be dealt with. Alternatively, where there is a significant dispute in relation to liability it may nonetheless be appropriate to seek settlement of quantum, though dealing with liability through a split trial, before embarking on quantum investigations, may prove more economical where quantum is complex.

Secondary Objectives

Claims may not fully settle at a JSM. Where this is the case, some benefit might still be achieved through the meeting if parties have in mind secondary objectives which, though they will not conclude the claim, might save time and cost in the future. Typically, there will be a hierarchy, such as the following;

1. Settle the claim or, failing that,

2. Settle liability, contributory negligence or quantum or,

3. Agree certain heads of loss or factual issues, or

4. Agree a roadmap or directions in order to get the evidence required to settle.

Not all of the objectives will be relevant to each JSM. It may not be tactically advisable to agree particular facts or heads of loss and if the only progress made is to agree further directions, then this is likely to be a sign that the JSM was poorly timed. However, the following example may help demonstrate how these can be useful.

A JSM is arranged in relation to a serious head injury claim. The claim includes a substantial claim for the costs of a deputy on the basis the claimant lacks capacity to manage his financial affairs. The expert evidence as to whether the claimant does lack capacity is conflicting and the parties are unable to agree on this element. Therefore they agree:

• *final settlement figures for all elements of the claim, save deputy fees*

• *quantum of the deputy fees, if the claimant does lack capacity*

- *a draft order providing for psychiatrists reports on capacity followed by a joint statement*

In the above example, the parties were able to significantly narrow the remaining issues through the JSM and agree the steps they would take to resolve the final area of dispute. Subject to approval, a substantial interim payment could reasonably have been agreed in addition, allowing the claimant the benefit of the majority of his damages without delay.

Is a JSM warranted by my case?

We started this chapter by considering the objectives of a JSM as this is a necessary precursor to the next question which is whether a JSM is appropriate on a particular case. Primarily, this question is determined by a consideration of whether the cost of a JSM is proportionate to the benefits offered, taking into account the value of the claim and the alternative ways of achieving the JSM objectives. .

The costs of a JSM vary widely, depending on the value and complexity of the case, but taking into account preparation time of both parties and cost of the meeting (which is often undertaken with counsel, though that is not necessary in all cases), a typical figure for a face to face JSM might be in the region of £10,000 per party. This does not include the costs which will be expended on evidence and documents used at the JSM. Therefore, for a JSM to be proportionate, the claim must have a significant value

Lord Justice Jackson's final report following his Review of Civil Litigation Costs suggests JSMs are better suited to claims of £500,000 upwards[1]. We agree this is where they add most value as a settlement tool, though they may be worth consideration in claims from around £250,000, particularly where there is scope to save significant litigation costs through an early resolution. Below that level, proportionality becomes increasingly problematic, though some of the modified "JSM"

---

1   Review of Civil Litigation Costs: Final Report, December 2009, p355

approaches mentioned at the end of this chapter may provide an effective settlement opportunity.

Before embarking on a JSM, alternatives must also be considered. For example, would it be equally feasible to negotiate by telephone, or settle via Part 36 offers? In lower value cases, where issues may be relatively straightforward, this may offer better value than a JSM. Alternatively, would mediation or arbitration be more appropriate?

There are very few, if any, cases which, by their nature, are unsuited to a JSM. Where liability is denied, this is an additional hurdle to settlement, but these claims can and do settle at JSMs. The reason for this, of course, is that each party understands their risk on liability and will be prepared to make concessions accordingly. Indeed, a Northern Circuit Working Party on JSMs in personal injury cases suggested that where a claimant has significant difficulty on liability, an early meeting may be appropriate with a view to compromising the claim in a manner proportionate to the risk, before costs escalate[2].

The most persuasive example, in our view, of a case in which a JSM may not be appropriate is a case in which there is an important point of principle at stake for one of the parties, or a case being run as a test case. Here a court decision may be of particular value to one or both of the parties.

Litigators should always be mindful of the courts' ability to impose costs penalties for failure to engage in a JSM, and where one is proposed, the default response should generally be to agree (with caveats on timing etc. where appropriate) or to suggest an alternative form of ADR if a JSM appears disproportionate.

---

2 Report of Northern Circuit Working Party on Joint Meetings in Personal injury cases, currently available at http://www.northerncircuit.org.uk/wp-content/uploads/2010/01/JSM-Report.pdf

The Timing of a JSM

JSMs typically take place after the commencement of court proceedings, though it would be wrong to suggest that litigation is necessary before a JSM can usefully take place.

The key to the timing of a JSM is to identify the earliest point at which there will be sufficient evidence and information available to both parties to engage in a meaningful negotiation in relation to the key issues standing in the way of settlement of the claim or issues that will be the subject of the meeting.

There is therefore a balance to be struck. On the one hand, an early, successful JSM may significantly reduce settlement time and save substantial costs. In this regard, recent increases to court fees provide an added incentive to seek settlement prior to proceedings. On the other, a JSM will be less likely to result in settlement if there is insufficient information available to the parties when it takes place as investigations are not complete.

In the next 2 sections, we will consider the evidence needed for a successful JSM and the need for a roadmap to allow this to be obtained.

Preparation for a JSM

<u>Roadmap to a JSM</u>

Once the parties agree to hold a JSM, it is important that they spend time agreeing the way in which they will prepare for it. This should include:

- identification of the issues to be considered at the JSM

- agreement on the evidence and information each party will exchange in relation to the issues

- timescales for exchange

- a review phase

- target JSM date.

The agreed roadmap should be recorded and shared by the parties, and the parties should keep it under review as preparations proceed. If additional issues arise, or there are delays, the parties should discuss the roadmap and make any necessary amendments as soon as possible.

There are no rules as to the format of a roadmap, or how it should be prepared. It may be agreed in a telephone call, or by correspondence. Where proceedings have been issued and case management is taking place, it may be recorded in directions. What is key is that both parties agree and record their plan to arrive at the JSM.

The following sections cover some of the steps which may go into a roadmap.

Knowing the claim

A JSM cannot take place unless each party is able to prepare with a good understanding of the other's position. If the information in the letter of claim and response (in a claim prior to court proceedings) or pleadings is not sufficiently comprehensive then the roadmap should include steps to address this.

The most common example of this in JSMs is the need for a full schedule of loss and counter schedule before a meeting takes place. Typically, these are one of the last steps before the meeting, allowing the documents to be prepared when all relevant evidence is available.

It is not at all uncommon for these to be exchanged at the very last minute, which can put a JSM at risk, prevent settlement or at least mean more drawn out negotiations than would otherwise be the case. By including the schedule and counter schedule in the roadmap, these risks can be reduced.

In other circumstances, a request for further particulars may be required. Within litigation, this might be achieved through a Part 18 request. There is no similar mechanism that can be deployed prior to issue, but if it is felt that additional information is needed in order to arrive at a JSM, then this might form part of the roadmap.

Evidence

Once the objectives of a JSM are understood and the issues are clear, it is possible to start considering the evidence needed to achieve those objectives. In doing so, consideration must be given to both the need for representatives to be able to advise and take instructions from their clients, and to engage in meaningful, constructive negotiations.

In an injury claim, expert medical evidence in relation to the most serious injuries will need to be completed before a JSM. It may be that both parties need to be given the opportunity to obtain a report, with a joint statement being prepared by the experts in order for a meeting to be effective.

Where there is a substantial care claim, a care report is likely to be required. The need for expert liability evidence, or reports in relation to treatment or losses will depend very much on the nature of the claim, and the availability of alternative information in support.

The need for witness statements also requires consideration. Where there is a dispute on liability (unless it is on a legal point) then statements are likely to be required, unless there is an alternative source of detailed witness information, such as a police or HSE investigation report.

Where the JSM is to deal with quantum only, the Schedule will set out alleged losses. A witness statement which simply replicates the assertions made in the schedule may add nothing to negotiations (though it would be required if the matter were to proceed to trial).

Disclosure of documentary evidence forms an important part of preparation for a JSM. This evidence is relatively quick and inexpensive to obtain and may answer many of the questions the parties have in relation to a case. By way of example, the tax returns of a self employed claimant may provide sufficient information for parties to calculate losses and negotiate a settlement even where an accountant's report would be justified if the matter were to go to trial.

Having the right evidence is key to an effective JSM, and it is important that in deciding what evidence is required that representatives consult both their client and the other party. The question of evidence must also be kept under review as preparations are made for a JSM. If a gap emerges, early action may allow it to be filled, or a JSM might be postponed while further investigation takes place.

The Review phase

It will always be prudent to allow some leeway between completion of evidence and a JSM. This allows contingency in the event preparation of any evidence is delayed. It also provides the opportunity for the parties and their clients to undertake a review before a JSM.

In high value cases, parties may each hold conferences at this stage, possibly with experts, in order to consider the evidence. In other cases the review may be less formal. What is important is that each party considers at this point whether they now have the information and evidence required to engage in a meaningful JSM.

It is rare, in our experience, for parties to wholly abandon the idea of a JSM at this stage. However, it is not unusual for parties to discover that new issues have arisen, or that they require some additional information or evidence before they go to a JSM. In many cases, this can be obtained quickly and the JSM proceeds as planned. In others, it may be necessary to postpone the JSM, for example in order to allow further expert evidence to be obtained.

The JSM

Attendees

It is essential that all those needed to make a settlement decision are available at a JSM. Therefore it will generally be attended by:

- the claimant

- a representative of the defendant insurer

- each party's solicitor

- counsel for each party

Others may be required, such as:

- the litigation friend where the claimant is a child or patient

- the defendant, particularly where liability is to be determined through a JSM or there is no insurance or a large excess

- reinsurers where the value of a claim is at a level which requires their involvement in the settlement decision

If leading counsel is instructed a junior may be present, and solicitors may bring assistants, however in our view this is rarely necessary, and the Courts are increasingly willing to disallow such costs when assessing bills.

It is rare for experts to be required at a JSM, though it does occur. Generally, it will be preferable to explore expert evidence through reports, questions and, where relevant, joint statements than to seek their opinion on the day. If a party plans to attend with an expert, they should inform the other party at the earliest opportunity so as to allow the other party to arrange attendance of their own expert.

Format of the meetings

Parties should each have a conference room at the JSM venue, with space for all those they attend with. There should also be a negotiating room.

A JSM will take place on a 'without prejudice' footing, meaning that the information and views exchanged may not be communicated to the Court.

There are no rules as to the agenda for a JSM, but the following is typical. In this example, we have assumed counsel is attending as well as solicitors. Of course, where one or more of the solicitors are undertaking the negotiations, they will be taking the role of counsel.

A typical JSM will begin with an opportunity for parties to hold their own conference. While advisors on each side ought already to have provided their substantive advice (whether on paper or in conference), this is an opportunity to refresh that advice, and discuss strategy for the meeting.

Counsel may also meet early on, in the negotiation room, to discuss the format for the day, and ground rules for negotiations, such as whether liability will be dealt with before quantum, whether offers will be net or gross of contributory negligence and who will be in the negotiating room.

Once these preliminaries are concluded, it will be time to commence the negotiations. These take place in the negotiating room, and typically are attended by only counsel for the parties or by counsel and their solicitors. It is rare for clients to also be present in the room.

When considering who should be in the negotiations, the question should be how to achieve the most effective negotiations. In our view the answer will often be to limit those present to counsel for each party. Injury claims may involve a significant amount of emotion for each party, and even their solicitors may not be immune to this. A counsel to counsel approach permits frank discussion between negotiators, who can then report back to their instructing solicitor and their client.

The first round of negotiations may or may not include an offer. Where parties require clarification of each others' case, or there are complex legal or factual issues to be explored, it may be preferable to explore these first, report back to the parties and then reconvene to take negotiations further. In straightforward cases, or those where the issues are clear, it may be possible to put an offer earlier on.

When the time does arrive for an offer, counsel will take instructions from their clients in their individual conference rooms. They will then re-join counsel for the other party to put the offer and discuss it. The other party may have a counter offer to put, or may take further instructions first.

At the meeting progresses, the interval between offers typically reduces, as all issues have been discussed and the focus shifts to whether a settlement is possible or not.

Terminating a JSM

A JSM should not lightly be cut short, but there are some circumstances in which it will be reasonable to do so.

Unfortunately, despite careful preparation, it sometimes happens that instructions taken on the day of a JSM uncover new issues. Examples include a claimant reporting deteriorating symptoms relating to an injury, or emerging risks such as a recent seizure which may indicate epilepsy attributable to a brain injury.

In such circumstances the legal representatives will need to consider whether it is feasible to attempt negotiation with this new information, or whether further investigations are necessary. If the planned negotiations cannot take place, secondary objectives (such as settlement of liability) may be possible, but in some cases the JSM will need to be terminated. In such cases there is a risk of costs sanctions (the costs of the

JSM having been incurred with no benefit). It is in part for this reason that the review phase is of such importance, as it minimises the risk of surprises at the JSM.

Conversely, one party may present a revised schedule or counter schedule, or otherwise introduce a new issue or evidence, shortly before or on the day of the morning of the meeting, with little or no justification. In such cases, the other party should consider whether they have the time and the evidence to deal with this new development. If so, it will be appropriate to proceed with the JSM. If not it may be appropriate to cancel or adjourn the JSM.

In relation to both of the examples above, parties should consider whether any secondary objectives for the JSM can be achieved, or whether the factor that has put the JSM at risk is one which can be 'parked' and investigated following the JSM, after other elements of the claim have been settled.

In other cases, a JSM has to be terminated because the parties simply are not making sufficient progress towards a settlement. If there is a substantial gap between offers and neither party appears to have more to give, there may be no benefit to proceeding with the JSM. In this situation, it is worth bearing in mind that many cases which do not settle at a JSM nonetheless settle shortly after. It may therefore be appropriate for a party to leave their final offer open for acceptance after the JSM (perhaps on a time limited basis, such as until 4pm or the end of the week).

Where there is a significant gap between offers, it will be appropriate to use the JSM to explore the reason, and to consider whether there is a means of resolving the issue or issue leading to the gap. For example, would obtaining further documents, an expert report or putting agreed questions to an expert resolve the point? Alternatively would there be any benefit to asking the court to determent the point through the trial of a preliminary issue?

<u>Wrapping up</u>

Where a JSM results in settlement of the issue or claim, the settlement terms should be written up and agreed at the conclusion of the meeting. Where the claim is litigated and terms are straightforward, this may be in the form of a final Consent Order. Where the order will be more complex (such as where Periodical Payments are part of the settlement) it will be preferable to limit this record to a note of the points agreed and draw up the Order following the meeting.

Where the claim does not settle, but progress has been made in relation to some issues, the parties may wish to consider whether those issues can be formally agreed. Once again, any such agreement should be recorded in writing.

In relation to claims which do not settle, or do not fully settle, the JSM provides an opportunity for representatives to meet with their client and counsel and discuss future strategy. For example, should the meeting be followed with a Part 36 offer? What evidence is required at this stage? Does the client need updating advice in relation to quantum or (as in the case of an insurer) reserves? Even in relation to settled cases, brief advice on any approval requirements, arrangement for payments and the process to resolve costs is likely to be beneficial.

JSMs and Part 36 offers

Practitioners sometimes express concern that the JSM process will be used by their opponent as an opportunity to make a Part 36 offer, which may adversely impact upon their client. The process of exchanging evidence and exploring each party's position certainly will involve the provision of evidence which would assist either party in making such an offer. However, that is the purpose of the process. It should be borne in mind that each party is likely to benefit to a similar extent, if a sensible roadmap is put in place, and they will be assisted both in making offers and in responding to any offers made to them.

JSMs involving multiple parties.

Multi-party claims are just as capable of resolution via a JSM as any other case, and indeed the costs associated with such claims should encourage parties to consider early dispute resolution via this or another route.

How a JSM will be approached will depend upon the issues between the parties, and their tactics in relation to a claim. The examples below will help illustrate this

Multi party liability disputes

Where, for example, a construction injury dispute involves multiple defendants involved in a project, with allegations of contributory negligence on the part of a claimant, a JSM with all parties participating can be a very effective means of resolving liability, with significant costs savings.

Of course, where quantum evidence is available, such a meeting may well resolve the whole claim.

Multi party claims: quantum only disputes

Where a claim involves multiple defendants but they may have already been able to agree their respective liabilities (defendant A to bear 30%, defendant B 20% and so on) the outstanding issue may simply be how much the defendants will jointly pay to the claimant. Here, negotiations will be most effective if they are bilateral – the claimant negotiating with the defendants as a group rather than with each of the defendants individually.

The defendants may nominate one of their number (typically the one with the greatest exposure) to take a lead on settlement negotiations. This assists in controlling costs for all parties and can speed up the negotiation process. In such cases the lead defendant should be careful to ensure all others are advised of intended offers and agree them, and have provided appropriate authorities so an effective JSM can take place and so as to avoid any argument of over settlement at a later date.

If such cooperation is not possible, defendants may still be able to instruct a single solicitor and/or barrister to represent all their interests, taking instructions from each of the defendants throughout the negotiating process.

Multiple Claimants

A variant of a JSM can also be used where multiple claimants are involved. For example, in a group action numerous claims may need to be negotiated. While each may have a limited value, overall it may be proportionate to arrange 'settlement days' where parties will meet to negotiate a number of claims, one after the other. A standard roadmap can be put in place, which each individual claim will follow prior to the meeting, to ensure all evidence is available before discussions take place.

In a group action, a number of these meetings may be held, perhaps at regular intervals, allowing claims to be negotiated as and when there is sufficient evidence to settle.

Alternative formats

The examples we have discussed above show the flexibility of a JSM, but in each case we have assumed that the core of the JSM will be a face to face meeting. This will not be proportionate in many personal injury cases, but money saving alternatives are possible.

Remote communication with client(s)

It is important that clients are available to give instructions on the day, but they do not necessarily have to attend the meeting. Being available by telephone or by video link would be sufficient in many cases. It is however essential that the client is truly available, and is in a position to take the time to understand advice and give instructions as and when needed.

Video Linked JSM

It is possible to replace the "negotiation room" with a video link between offices. This may be of particular assistance where parties are based in locations remote from one another, although unless there are significant costs savings, we would suggest it is better for the negotiations to be face to face and take instructions remotely.

Telephone negotiations

Even in a claim of relatively modest value, something can be taken from the JSM model to make telephone negotiations more effective.

Being able to agree a time to negotiate, at which all parties can engage (via conference call if necessary) and with a simple process for exchange of any documents on which they will rely is likely to focus parties' minds upon settlement and lead to a more structured and productive negotiation than an ad-hoc call.

For example, liability disputes in lower value injury claims might be resolved via a multi-party telephone conference call between all representatives.

Court control over JSMs

The Courts have limited power to impose ADR, but through case management orders can direct the parties towards ADR and can impose sanctions on parties who fail to engage.

The Directions Questionnaire[3] therefore includes a questions as to whether representatives have advised their clients of the need to settle, whether parties want to attempt settlement at this stage and if so whether a 1 month stay is requested for this purpose. If parties say they do not wish to settle then they are to set out reasons.

---

3   Form N181

CPR 26.4 then requires the court to grant a stay of 1 month when all parties request it, and allows the court to grant a stay of 1 month or such period as seems appropriate, where the court considers it appropriate to do so.

Therefore, from the outset the court process requires consideration of ADR, including JSMs, with direction available in order to facilitate it.

Practice direction to Part 29, paragraph 4.10(9) indicates that where appropriate the Court may give direction for parties to consider ADR, and proposes the following wording for such a direction:

> *"The parties shall by [date] consider whether the case is capable of resolution by ADR. If any party considers that the case is unsuitable for resolution by ADR, that party shall be prepared to justify that decision at the conclusion of the trial, should the judge consider that such means of resolution were appropriate, when he is considering the appropriate costs order to make.*

> *The party considering the case unsuitable for ADR shall, not less than 28 days before the commencement of the trial, file with the court a witness statement without prejudice save as to costs, giving reasons upon which they rely for saying that the case was unsuitable."*

Such a direction is frequently part of multi track orders, and ensure the onus is on the party refusing ADR to explain their position (as they are required to do in the direction questionnaire). As set out above, there are few claims in which ADR will not be appropriate and therefore careful consideration should be given to a request for ADR and time taken to ensure the reasons given for any refusal are cogent.

However, as we have also demonstrated, a JSM is only likely to be effective when adequate preparation has taken place, and a party is unlikely to be criticised if they (with good reason) respond to the effect that it is premature to engage in ADR as key evidence or information is missing. Where this is the response, it will generally be beneficial for that party to propose an outline of a roadmap allowing for that evidence to be obtained and ADR to take place at a later date.

Where the court is case managing a case, the roadmap will typically be reflected in directions, which may allow for exchange of evidence followed by a stay to permit the parties to consider and engage in ADR. In other cases a longer stay may be granted, without directions for exchange of evidence, on the basis the parties will engage in preparation for a JSM (or other ADR) without the need for a court timetable. In such cases it is important the parties do make real progress, or they may face criticism from the court, notwithstanding the fact they have not missed any formal directions.

Enforcement of ADR related orders is achieved through costs sanctions. In Christian -v- The Commission of Police for the Metropolis [2015] EWHC 371 (QB), though the defendant was wholly successful, it was denied one third of its assessed costs, having disregarded numerous requests to engage in a settlement meeting. The judge determined that ADR did have a reasonable prospect of success and ought to have been attempted. The defendant had declined to do so with inadequate (or inadequately articulated) reason, and in such circumstances a costs sanction was appropriate.

Summary

- Joint Settlement meetings are an effective settlement tool in higher value claims where the cost of a JSM is proportionate to the issues.

- Establishing clear objectives for a JSM and a roadmap to ensure the necessary evidence and information will be available at the JSM is key to a successful meeting

- Roadmaps should be reviewed on an ongoing basis to ensure that the evidence gathering process and timetable remain appropriate.

- The JSM itself typically follows a format of parties meeting with their representatives alternating with counsel to counsel negotiations.

- Considering secondary objectives (such as agreeing issues or a strategy to resolve blocks to settlement) helps ensure that a JSM which does not end is settlement of the claim or issues intended to be addressed may nonetheless achieve meaningful progress.

- Parties are at risk of cost penalties if they refuse to engage in ADR, including proposals for a JSM, without good reason.

CHAPTER TEN
ARBITRATION AND
ADJUDICATION

Commercial arbitrations have a long history, due to a variety of factors including industry specific schemes, arbitration clauses written into the contracts from which disputes arise and the benefits of maintaining commercial confidentiality and relationships through the process.

Arbitration in personal injury claims has yet to gain the same traction, though with increasing court fees, and dissatisfaction in relation to some court processes (such as costs budgeting[1]) and delays, this may change in coming years, as part of an increased drive towards ADR.

In this chapter, we will begin by considering ways in which issues might be resolved by referral to an independent third party. We will then go on to outline the manner in which true arbitration might be adopted as a stand alone method by which to resolve a claim. We will not attempt to give a full account of the law of arbitration, but to demonstrate the features which might be applied within the context of personal injury ADR.

Key features of Arbitration

How does Mediation or a JSM differ from Arbitration?

Arbitration is a form of compulsory process. An arbitration agreement can be made in one of two ways. First, parties to a contract may have agreed in advance that in the event that a dispute arises between them, that dispute should be referred to arbitration according to a particular system of law and a particular procedure. Secondly, there may be an ad hoc reference to arbitration after a dispute has arisen. If there is a bind-

---

1 One Personal Injury Arbitration provider advertises the ability to avoid budgeting and associated costs as a particular advantage of their scheme, though there is no reason in principle why budgeting cannot take place during an arbitration process, using Arbitrators powers under s65 of the Arbitration Act 1996.

ing agreement the parties can be compelled to participate, on risk of penalty.

Control of process - orders

Under English law, notably the Arbitration Act 1996, and under most arbitration procedural rules, the arbitration tribunal will be the master of the process and will have authority over the parties in certain respects (supported by the English Court where necessary). This will generally permit the arbitration tribunal to make orders, like setting down the timetable for the arbitration process and compelling the parties to comply with that timetable. Another example; the arbitration tribunal may, generally on the application of one of the parties, order that certain categories of document should be disclosed in the proceedings. In the event that they are not, the arbitrators may be at liberty to impose penalties. This is quite unlike mediation.

Privacy

Arbitration is private and this is one reason why many commercial bodies prefer that their disputes are always referred to arbitration. There is then less risk that any element of the arbitration will find its way into the public domain. The names of the parties, the issues at stake, the pleadings, the underlying documents, any witness statements, any experts reports and moreover the Arbitration Award itself; few of these are ever likely to see the light of day. In this respect arbitration and mediation are similar, but certainly not identical. The key difference is that there is no guarantee that arbitration proceedings will remain private. If an Award can be appealed, then the trial of that appeal will, save in the most unusual circumstances, be public and the names of the parties and perhaps all of the issues between them will then find their way into the public domain. An Award may equally become public through an enforcement process or through pursuit of an indemnity claim.

Decision making - award

Arbitration (like litigation) is a decision making process. At the end of the process, at the conclusion of the arbitration hearing, the arbitration tribunal will make findings of fact and conclusions of law and thereby reach an adjudication on the issues between the parties.

Enforcement

There is also the issue of enforcement. Obtaining an Arbitration Award, or even a judgment, is not necessarily the end of the story. In personal injury claims, however, the defendant is normally backed by insurance.

Arbitration Awards can be readily enforced in England and Wales as a judgment and abroad under the 1958 New York Convention. But despite the many advantages of arbitration, it suffers from certain shortcomings. Indeed, these are the very factors both in litigation and arbitration which prompted the original development and latterly the growth in the use of commercial mediation.

Win/lose scenarios

There is always risk in litigation or arbitration. The prospects of success or failure in any particular case can be assessed (in some measure) at various stages, but new documents and information often emerge during the course of the dispute and one can never predict with certainty how an expert or a factual witness might perform at a final trial nor what final Award (or Judgment) will be given. A significant amount of time and cost can be devoted to a dispute before surprises emerge. However, the ultimate outcome of an arbitration (like litigation) will typically be a win/loose scenario – there is no scope for an arbitrator to explore middle ground taking into account risk – an arbitrator, like a judge must make a decision.

Adjudication on an issue

We have discussed in the preceding chapters situations in which forms of ADR may lead to resolution of some but not all issues in a claim. In those circumstances, the parties may be able to call on a neutral third party to resolve the outstanding issue(s) for them, in order to conclude the case.

This typically applies where there is a question of law or of expert opinion to be determined, where the parties can present an agreed set of background facts, and invite a specialist to draw conclusions on the basis of these. This is not true arbitration, but borrows some features of an arbitration process and is a useful tool in resolving disputes, and one that can be readily deployed at limited cost, in appropriate cases.

Referral to an independent legal advisor on a question of law

It is relatively rare for significant disputes of law to arise in personal injury claims, but where they do they can pose a significant impediment to resolution of a claim. In such cases, court proceedings may prove costly and the court process may lead to unnecessary delay. Referral to a mutually agreed independent adjudicator may provide a more cost effective and timely determination of the issue, which may permit the parties to resolve the claim.

One such example may be the test for recovery of damages in nervous shock claims[2]. In such cases, parties may agree the factual circumstances and that a psychological injury has arisen, but disagree on whether the legal test for recovery of damages is satisfied. A neutral personal injury QC provided with an agreed summary of facts, medical report and submissions from the parties will be able to provide a decision as to whether the claim succeeds.

Such an approach may also assist in resolving issues between particular parties, such as when there is a dispute as to interpretation of contracts determining defendants' relationships (and so liabilities) or in relation to insurers' liabilities where multiple potentially relevant policies exist.

---

2   Nervous shock claims (see for example *Liverpool Women's Hospital NHS Foundation Trust v Ronayne* [2015] EWCA Civ 588) relate to individuals suffering psychological injury having witnessed an incident or its aftermath. In order to recover damages, claimants must show they satisfy a proximity test particular to this class of negligence claims.

Referral to an expert on a question of opinion

In a similar manner to the examples provided above, a decision on an issue of expert evidence may be required in order to resolve a claim. For example, whether the claimant has capacity to manage his or her affairs may determine whether deputyship costs are payable, or the parties may dispute the correct interpretation of information in relation to historic accounts or tax liabilities. In such circumstances, an agreed, neutral expert (in these two examples a psychiatrist and accountant, respectively) agreed by the parties might be asked to address the issue and report to the parties with an opinion.

Terms for adjudication on issues

Where neutral adjudications of the type set out above are used, parties have broad flexibility to agree the terms on which the process will take place. Terms will depend upon the issue to be decided, the nature of the case, the parties interests and the need to resolve the issue at proportionate costs. They would typically cover:

- The question to be determined

- Applicable law

- A process for preparation of a written set of agreed facts, as a basis for the process.

- Evidence (if any) to be submitted to the decision maker

- Any powers for the decision maker to request evidence or obtain evidence (such as through a medical examination)

- Process for parties to make submissions to the decision maker (which may be in writing or oral)

- Form of decision – is a fully reasoned 'judgement' required, or a decision with a brief summary of reasons?

- Whether the decision will be treated as binding.

- Costs of the process – will the decision maker be paid on a fixed costs basis?

- Who will be liable for those costs?

- Costs of the case – if the process will determine the claim, what will the costs consequences be?

- Are the documents prepared for the process and/or decision to be treated as being 'without prejudice' and/or confidential both in relation to the present claim and any other related claims?

It will be noted that the decision maker may be asked to give a non-binding opinion. Essentially, this would amount to the parties obtaining an early neutral evaluation. Though not binding, this may assist them in the course of further investigation and/or negotiation of the claim.

Arbitration of Claims

As with adjudication of issues, there is significant scope for parties to personal injury claims to determine the terms on which arbitration will take place. However, arbitration of a claim is different in that there may be numerous issues to be determined and a requirement for a number of evidence gathering steps before a final decision, and the arbitrator has a role in managing the process as well as determining its outcome. It is an alternative process to litigation in the courts, which may include mandatory steps akin to those in litigation, and also other forms of ADR before the arbitrator determines the case.

Arbitration provided by an arbitration service

Arbitration services have developed their own models of arbitration with standard contracts and processes, and panels of specialist arbitrators. Such services will offer a fee structure which may be fixed, based on a simple hourly rate or may be staged to include, for example, commencement costs, costs of interventions by the arbitrator during the process and costs of an arbitration hearing. In this respect the personal injury claims sector is somewhat behind commercial dispute resolution, with no well established arbitration body in place though providers are emerging and this may become a growth industry.

One model for personal injury arbitration, which is available at present, mirrors key parts of the court process, but promises more procedural freedom for the parties, lower costs and less delay. A standard arbitration agreement and process map provides for parties to sign up to the service (with an initial cost) after which they will exchange pleadings and evidence, according to a timetable they may agree, with a view to a hearing before the arbitrator. Parties may request extensions of time from the arbitrator at any stage, and may make a complaint against their opponent for untoward delays. The process may include early evaluation of the claim by the arbitrator and a JSM in order to encourage settlement before the arbitration hearing takes place. Fees are a combination of fixed fees and hourly rates.

This is not the only model available, and different providers are likely to offer alternatives processes and pricing structures.

Bespoke arbitration agreements

Parties may wish to use the flexibility of arbitration to design their own agreement to suit their priorities in relation to a particular claim. An arbitrator or arbitrators will, of course, need to be identified to make the award and, so far as permitted by the agreement, to intervene during the arbitration process. However, a well-crafted agreement will be required, and both parties must be prepared to sign up to its terms and to agree an arbitrator or means of appointing one. Parties who elect to pursue this course will require a good knowledge of arbitration law.

Pre Arbitration Steps

Parties may also seek to complete evidential steps and some form of ADR prior to arbitration. In personal injury claims it may well be appropriate to follow the pre action protocols prior to arbitration, in the same way as would be expected prior to litigation. Parties may go further and proceed to a mediation or JSM, only going to arbitration if this does not result in settlement. This may limit the steps the parties need to take during arbitration, resulting in a shorter and more cost effective process.

Terms for arbitration on Claims

As can be seen from the above, use of arbitration as a form of ADR may range from use of a service with standard terms to a bespoke agreement, and may involve an arbitrator managing a case in a manner similar to a judge or may rely on parties to agree a timetable. It is the flexibility that is available in arbitration which is part of its appeal.

It is therefore necessary that parties apply themselves carefully to the task of considering their arbitration agreement, in order to ensure the terms suit the claim and their objectives. The following section which explains the framework within which arbitration takes place will demonstrate some key aspects for parties to consider when entering into an arbitration agreement.

The Arbitration Act 1996

The Arbitration Act 1996 sets out the law governing arbitrations. The Act applies where the seat of the arbitration is in England and Wales or Northern Ireland[3], and where the arbitration agreement is in writing[4]. In this respect, "agreement in writing" is given a broad interpretation so as to include, for example, agreements recorded in writing. Under the Act, the parties may agree when the arbitration process is deemed to

---

3   Arbitration Act 1996 s2

4   Ibid s 5

have commenced, but otherwise it will be treated as having commenced when an arbitrator is identified, or when one party gives notice to the other requiring them to appoint an arbitrator[5]

The Act is a lengthy piece of legislation, which is the subject of other specialist textbooks. The following is therefore limited to an outline which it is hoped will be useful in considering the use of arbitration in civil claims.

Mandatory provisions

The Act recognises that parties should be free to agree on how to resolve their disputes, subject to safeguards in the public interest and therefore leaves significant latitude for parties to design an arbitration to suit their needs. There are, nonetheless, some elements of which parties entering into arbitration agreements should be aware. The Act sets out only a limited number of mandatory provisions which will apply irrespective of any agreement to the contrary between the parties. These include:

- The duty of the tribunal to act fairly and impartially and to adopt procedures suitable to the case[6] and of the parties to do "all things necessary for the proper and expeditious conduct" of the arbitration[7]

- Provisions in relation to staying of legal proceedings while arbitration takes place[8]

- The Court's ability to extend the time for commencement of arbitration[9]

---

5 Ibid s 14
6 Ibid s 33
7 Ibid s 40
8 Ibid s 9 - 11
9 Ibid s 12

- Provisions in relation to limitation, which applies in arbitration proceedings as in legal proceedings, but in relation to which the time taken in an arbitration subsequently set aside or found to be no effect may be disregarded by the court. [10]

- the court's powers to remove an arbitrator [11] or hear a challenge to an award[12] in certain circumstances,

- the court's ability rule on the arbitrator's jurisdiction[13], or hear a challenge in relation to the agreement, constitution of the tribunal or the matters submitted to arbitration, by a party not taking part in the proceedings[14] (which may be lost where a party does take part[15])

- the process for dealing with issues in relation to the arbitrator's jurisdiction[16]

- the parties' joint and several liability in relation to the arbitrator's fees and expenses reasonably incurred [17], including those of experts, legal advisors and assessors[18], and the arbitrators ability to refuse to deliver an award pending receipt of fees[19]. Parties may agree that one or other is to pay the whole cost of the arbitration, though only after the dispute has arisen[20]

---

10 Ibid s 13
11 Ibid s 24
12 Ibid s 67 and 68
13 Ibid s 32
14 Ibid s 72
15 Ibid s 73
16 Ibid s 31
17 Ibid s 28
18 Ibid s37(2)
19 Ibid s 56
20 Ibid s 60

- in relation to the death or an arbitrator[21]

- the immunity of the arbitrator[22] and arbitration providers[23] from claims, save for acts or omissions in bad faith

- Court powers to enforce an arbitration award[24]

Arbitration arrangements

In addition to the mandatory provisions above, the Act sets out various provisions which will apply to an arbitration unless parties agree to the contrary. This includes provisions in relation to the number of arbitrators who will decide the issue (the tribunal) and appointment of arbitrators, a chairman and/or umpire. In most personal injury claims, a single arbitrator is likely to be adequate.

Arbitrators' procedural powers

The Act also provides an arbitrator with power to decide procedural matters, subject to the right of the parties to agree any procedural matter themselves (this should be dealt with in their agreement). These are set out at s 34 of the Act and include:

(a) when and where any part of the proceedings is to be held;

(b) the language or languages to be used in the proceedings and whether translations of any relevant documents are to be supplied;

(c) whether any and if so what form of written statements of claim and defence are to be used, when these should be supplied and the extent to which such statements can be later amended;

---

21 Ibid s 26(1)
22 Ibid s 29
23 Ibid s 74
24 Ibid s 66

(d) whether any and if so which documents or classes of documents should be disclosed between and produced by the parties and at what stage;

(e) whether any and if so what questions should be put to and answered by the respective parties and when and in what form this should be done;

(f) whether to apply strict rules of evidence (or any other rules) as to the admissibility, relevance or weight of any material (oral, written or other) sought to be tendered on any matters of fact or opinion, and the time, manner and form in which such material should be exchanged and presented;

(g) whether and to what extent the tribunal should itself take the initiative in ascertaining the facts and the law;

(h) whether and to what extent there should be oral or written evidence or submissions.

The same section permits the arbitrator to fix (and subsequently extend) deadlines by which any directions given are to be complied with. Sanctions are available to the arbitrator under s 41 of the Act including, in the case of inordinate and inexcusable delay which may render it impossible to fairly resolve an issue or which prejudices a party, dismissal of the claim. It will be noted that this is a high bar, when compared the civil courts' ability to impose sanctions for non-compliance. The arbitrator also has discretion on costs and in principle might impose costs sanctions if it appears it is not appropriate for the whole or part of costs to follow the event[25]

Parties may, with the permission of the arbitrator, summons a witness to attend before the arbitrator in order to give oral evidence or produce

---

25 Ibid s 61

documents, in a manner similar to the use of a witness summons in court proceedings[26]

The arbitrator is permitted by s 37 to appoint experts, legal advisors or assessors in relation to a claim, unless otherwise agreed by the parties. The associated fees and expenses are treated as expenses of the arbitrator, which must ultimately be borne by the parties, if reasonable. In relation to an injury claim, parties may wish to adopt the more familiar model of obtaining their own expert evidence, though there may be circumstances in which appointment of an expert or assessor by the arbitrator is advantageous. This power may therefore be constrained through the arbitration agreement.

It should be noted that while the Act provides procedural powers similar to those available to the court, this does not mean that an arbitration is bound to follow comparable processes. It is open to an arbitrator to adopt a more inquisitorial approach and/or to minimise procedure (subject always to the terms agreed between the parties) which may allow time and/or costs savings to be achieved. However, it should be borne in mind that in the sphere of personal injury claims, many of the issues will turn upon matters of fact and expert opinion and for a successful arbitration to take place it is important that the relevant evidence on these matters is obtained and made available to the parties and arbitrator.

Appeals from Arbitrations and intervention by the Courts

The Arbitration Act provides that the court should not intervene in arbitrations, except as provided in the Act.[27] This is in keeping with the objective of giving the parties latitude to determine how their dispute is resolved, and with the concept of arbitration as a separate process from litigation.

---

26 Ibid s 43
27 Ibid s 1(c)

The Court may intervene in order to consider the validity of the arbitration agreement, the jurisdiction of the tribunal and in relation to any allegation of irregularity (see further 'mandatory provisions' above).

Unless parties agree otherwise, the Court may also be used to decide a preliminary point of law[28] and to secure interim orders such as interim injunctions or orders for preservation of evidence[29]. The Court also retains the final say on the law, unless the agreement states otherwise, with appeal on points of law governed by s 69, which sets out the circumstances in which leave to appeal will be granted.

Enforcement

S 66 of the Act provides that an award arising from arbitration may be enforced via the court in the same manner as a judgment or order, with leave of the Court, save that leave will not be given when it is shown the tribunal lacked jurisdiction to make the award.

Summary

- Arbitration offers a flexible framework for resolution of claims, which may mirror or depart from the Court process as much or as little as the parties and (where empowered to decide) arbitrator consider appropriate

- The culmination of the arbitration (and some procedural aspects) will be determined by the arbitrator. The arbitration itself therefore offers little scope for compromise or "win-win" solutions which may be available under other forms of ADR.

- However, engaging in an arbitration process should not be seen as excluding other forms of ADR. For example, early neutral evaluation or a JSM may be allowed for.

---

28 Ibid s 45

29 Ibid s 44

- Arbitration agreements are generally be binding (subject to rights of appeal) and can be enforced.

- The increase in court fees increases the attractiveness of arbitration, as it offers a model which may be more cost effective, depending on the offerings developed by providers in coming years.

CHAPTER ELEVEN
COURT POWERS TO ORDER ADR, REASONS TO REFUSE ADR AND PENALTIES

As we have seen, the pre action protocols and associated practice direction are designed to create an opportunity for ADR, and emphasise the court's ability to penalise a party who unreasonably refuses. The Court can also order a stay for ADR during the proceedings, a sign that the Court expects parties to engage and a clear signal that penalties may follow if either does not. In anticipation of such an outcome, the Court may also order any party which fails to engage in ADR to provide a statement setting out reasons, which will be used when costs arguments are to be heard. The significance of the role of alternative dispute resolution and the obligation on the parties to consider ADR before and during the litigation process is further reinforced by the Jackson ADR Handbook (Oxford University Press (2013)).

The Court can then consider the position at the end of the case and consider with hindsight whether a party should be penalised in costs for refusing to engage in ADR.

When the court comes to consider costs and to exercise its discretion under Civil Procedure Rule 44.2, it has regard to all the circumstances, including the conduct of the parties before as well as during the proceedings (CPR 44.2 (4) and (5)). That includes whether a party refuses to agree to alternative dispute resolution.

As we have seen, part 36 offers may carry automatic costs consequences. In addition, one of the factors which the court will have regard to when exercising its powers as to costs is 'any admissible offer to settle made by a party which is drawn to the court's attention, and which is not an offer to which costs consequences under part 36 apply' (CPR 44.2(4)(c)). The range of potential litigation offers is reviewed in the earlier chapter on Part 36.

There is now a long line of cases demonstrating that the Courts will penalise parties who refuse to engage in ADR, beginning with the seminal case of Halsey v Milton Keynes NHS Trust [2004] EWCA (Civ) 576.

To avoid penalties being imposed, it is wise to offer to try ADR at the beginning as this puts the opponent under pressure to settle or face the consequences in terms of costs penalties, and to make appropriate offers at an early stage.

CPR 44.4 sets out the particular matters the Court will consider in relation to a costs order.—

> *(3) The court will also have regard to—*
>
> *(a) the conduct of all the parties, including in particular—*
>
> *(i) conduct before, as well as during, the proceedings; and*
>
> *(ii) the efforts made, if any, before and during the proceedings in order to try to resolve the dispute;....*

It is clear following **Halsey** and subsequent decisions that a refusal to mediate without good reason or justification will result in an adverse costs order, because it constitutes unreasonable conduct.

In Halsey, the Court gave the following list of potentially reasonable reasons for refusing:

• the nature of the dispute;

• the merits of the case;

• the extent to which other settlement methods have been attempted;

• whether ADR costs would be disproportionately high;

- would delay in setting up ADR have been prejudicial;

- whether the mediation had reasonable prospects of success.

Following the suggestion in the ADR Handbook that Halsey should be revisited, the Court of Appeal made it clear that the Halsey guidelines are not exhaustive and that the Court will look at the conduct of the parties at the time, from a subjective point of view. This was set out in the case of **PGF ii SA – v – OMFS Company Limited [2013] EWCA CIV 1288.**

The claim involved a property dispute. Initial proceedings claimed £1.81 million. The claim settled by the claimant's acceptance of the defendant's Part 36 offer to pay £700,000. The offer had been made approximately 12 months before trial but was accepted only one day before trial, during which period the Defendant had accumulated costs of approximately £250,000. However, the claimant had twice invited the defendant to mediate, which invitations had been met with silence. The Court of Appeal upheld an order that the defendant was not entitled to recover its costs for the period after the part 36 offer as the silence amounted to a refusal to mediate and neither the part 36 offer nor the gap between the parties' figures was adequate justification for this.

Reasons to refuse ADR

The courts consider that opportunities to engage in ADR should be taken up, and that any party refusing to do so or failing to respond may be penalised in costs. Below, we look at specific potential justifications identified in Halsey and consider the Court's current approach.

The nature of the dispute

In Garritt-Critchley and Others v Ronnan and Solarpower PV Limited, His Honour Judge Waksman QC rejected the submission that the dispute was unsuitable for mediation because it *"is not a claim which provides any natural middle ground between the parties."*

He said *"But that is usually the case on liability: it usually is a binary issue. There may be various liability outcomes in a more complex case but in a simple case the question is going to be, "Was there a breach of duty of care? Was there a breach of contract? Was there a contract?"; and so on and so forth. To consider that mediation is not worth it because the sides are opposed on a binary issue, I'm afraid seems to me to be misconceived."*

In Laporte & Anor v The Commissioner of Police of the Metropolis the defendant argued that the case was unsuitable for mediation because the claimants were seeking to litigate a point of legal principle concerning the scope of police powers.

Turner J rejected the argument saying: *"In my view, this was not a case in which the nature of the dispute made it unsuitable for mediation. The claimants could have succeeded in obtaining some level of damages even if they had lost on the law and even if, in addition, the actions of the inspector had been vindicated. There were issues of pure fact to be resolved about what happened on the staircase upon which both sides ran the risk of adverse findings. There was no continuing commercial relationship between the parties and it is unrealistic to suggest that a settlement by way of ADR would have been inappropriate for this type of dispute."*

In Rana v Tears of Sutton Bridge the successful defendant had refused mediation and gave the fact that liability was in dispute as a reason for refusing to mediate. His Honour Judge McKenna disallowed 40% of their costs saying: *"I am not impressed by their arguments that simply because liability was still in issue an attempt at alternative dispute resolution should not have taken place."*

A liability dispute between the parties will not in itself justify a refusal to engage in ADR.

We suggest that the position in relation to an offer to mediate or attend a JSM may be different where the outcome turns on an issue outside the parties' knowledge, for example where expert evidence is determinative. However this should not amount to a good reason to refuse to engage in ADR. It should be possible to use ADR to narrow the issues or move towards obtaining the necessary opinion, or adjudication by an expert may be possible.

The merits of the case or offer

The Court rejected the suggestion that merits alone could justify a refusal to mediate in Lynn v Borneos LLP t/a Borneo Linnels, saying *"The defendants simply did not respond or made fairly bland refusal to all the invitations to mediate. The effect pf authority is now, in my view, that the court should regard a refusal or a failure to engage a mediation in those circumstances as unreasonable. It is something which is, in principle, unreasonable no matter what the strength of a party's case is felt to be.*

Nor is the strength of an existing offer amount to good reason. In PGF II SA v OMFS Company 1 Ltd, the Appellant submitted that making a Part 36 offer of £700,000 *"and leaving it there until trial without subsequent adjustment, was a living demonstration of the defendant's belief in the strength of its case, a belief which, since the claimant eventually accepted it, cannot have been otherwise than reasonable".*

The Court rejected this argument saying *"it is in my view simply wrong to regard a Part 36 offer, without any supporting explanation for its basis, as a living demonstration of a party's belief in the strength of its case. As I have said, defendants' Part 36 offers are frequently made at a level below that which the defendant fears having to pay at trial, in the hope that the claimant's appetite for, or ability to undertake, costs risk will encourage it to settle for less than its claim is worth."*

In Garritt-Critchley and Others v Ronnan and Solarpower PV Limited, the Court observed that a party's belief in the strength of its case is not always an accurate appraisal in any event.

The court did not consider it reasonable for the defendant to be so confident in its case. It noted that no application for summary judgment had been made. The judge said that *"The fact that a party believes that he has a watertight case again is no justification for refusing mediation. That is the frame of mind of so many litigants."*

The justification argument based upon the 'merits' is not wholly without weight. In Northrop Grumman Mission Systems Europe Ltd v BAE Systems (Al Diriyah C4I) Ltd (No 2) the Court acknowledged the defendant's belief in the merits of its case but found that was only limited justification for not mediating and imposed a penalty. He said: *"....It was a case where BAE reasonably considered that it had a strong case As stated in Halsey, the fact that a party reasonably believes that it has a watertight case may well be sufficient justification for a refusal to mediate."*

However, he qualified this by observing *"The authors of the Jackson ADR Handbook properly, in my view, draw attention at paragraph 11.13 to the fact that this seems to ignore the positive effect that mediation can have in resolving disputes even if the claims have no merit. As they state, a mediator can bring a new independent perspective to the parties if using evaluative techniques and not every mediation ends in payment to a claimant.* Balancing these two considerations resulted in the conclusion that while BAE's srrong case provided some justification for not mediating, this was limited and overall was not sufficiently strong to justify the refusal, resulting in a finding of unreasonable conduct.

<u>The extent to which other settlement methods have been attempted</u>

If there has been a thorough well-intentioned attempt at settlement using on ADR, there may be some prospect of persuading the court that it is not reasonable to expect the parties then go on to attempt another. This argument, however, is not without risk. An initial attempt at ADR may reveal the fact that an alternative form has better chances of success.

In Reed Executive Plc v Reed Business Information Limited, mediation had been offered, but in response a party submitted that refusal was justified because it had been engaged in "serious settlement negotiations". The Court considered that such negotiations were not the same as mediation as "a good and tough mediator can bring about a sense of commercial reality to both sides which their own lawyers, however good, may not be able to convey."

The fact that both parties have made Part 36 offers has also been held not to be a sufficient reason. Mediators can provide anecdotal evidence that it is not all uncommon to see a case settle at mediation where there has previously been a round table or joint settlement meeting which did not produce a settlement.

<u>Whether the costs of the ADR would be disproportionately high</u>

In Garritt-Critchley and Others v Ronnan and Solarpower PV Limited the defendant refused to mediate on the basis that the costs of the mediation were likely to be as much as their latest offer to settle (£10,000). The judge described the argument as misconceived and said "*The point is that you compare the costs of a mediation with the costs of a trial. And the costs of a mediation, on any view, would have been far less than the costs of the trial, as both parties' costs figures demonstrate.*"

In practice, it is likely that ADR can always be undertaken at a cost which will be less than the alternative of a trial.

<u>Whether any delay in setting up and attending the ADR would have been prejudicial</u>

It is quite difficult to conceive of circumstances where the delay in setting up and attending ADR would in fact be prejudicial.

In Elliott Group Ltd (2) Algeco SAS and others, the court said that there would rarely be circumstances where a court would be willing to adjourn a trial so the parties can use ADR. In CIP Properties (AIPT) Ltd v Galliford Try Infrastructure Ltd Coulson J. said "*A stay or a fixed 'window' (for mediation) is likely to lead to delay, extra cost and uncertainty, and should not ordinarily be ordered.*"

By contrast, the court may, when giving directions, bear in mind that the rigours of case management should not prejudice the opportunity to explore ADR (Electrical Waste Recycling Group Ltd v Philips Electronics UK Ltd). Similarly, in CIP Properties (see above), the Court considered that "*A timetable for trial that allows the parties to take part in ADR along the way is a sensible case management tool.*" This was the conclusion of Briggs LJ in his Chancery Modernisation. Timetabling to trial and case management can result in an incentive to engage in ADR.

In practice (as the pre action protocols suggest) parties are considering ADR at the earliest opportunity.

<u>Whether the ADR had a reasonable prospect of success</u>

In PGF II SA v OMFS Company 1 Ltd30 the Appellant " *submitted that, mainly because of the monetary distance between the parties' respective Part 36 offers, both of which he characterised as their respective bottom lines, mediation stood no reasonable prospect of success.*

Briggs LJ rejected the argument. He said *"Nor do Part 36 offers necessarily or even usually represent the parties' respective bottom lines. There was, accordingly, no unbridgeable gulf between these parties' respective Part 36 offers, which could not in any circumstances have been overcome in a mediation.*

The court ordered a costs sanction in Lynn v Borneos LLP t/a Borneo Linnels despite the Court finding that " *nothing I have seen suggests to me that there would have been any realistic hope that the matter would have settled at mediation I think, realistically, I must approach this on the footing that, whilst it cannot be said there was no value in going to mediation, I cannot assume that there was a high possibility that there would have been a settlement achieved at any recognisable point in time which would have saved a significant amount of costs in preparation for the trial."*

In Garritt-Critchley and Others v Ronnan and Solarpower PV Limited the judge rejected the defendant's belief that the parties were too far apart for a mediation to be successful. He said *"Parties don't know whether in truth they are too far apart unless they sit down and explore settlement. If they are irreconcilably too far apart, then the mediator will say as much within the first hour of mediation. That happens very rarely in my experience."*

Insufficient Information

In Rana v Tears of Sutton Bridge the successful defendant refused to engage in ADR on grounds, amongst others, that there was insufficient information as to the quantification of the loss of profits claim and that disclosure had not taken place. The Judge said: *"I am not impressed by their arguments that simply because liability was still in issue and because there was not sufficient information as to the quantification of the loss of profits claim, still less that disclosure had not taken place, an attempt at alternative dispute resolution should not have taken place."* Taking everything into consideration the judge disallowed 40% of the defendant's costs.

Is this authority for the view that insufficient information is an inadequate reason to refuse ADR? It is worth noting there were a number of failings, as mentioned above, and it was also found that the Defendant had also failed to properly follow the pre action protocol. A Defendant denying liability should have limited interest in the precise quantification of, for example, loss of profits, as it can be assumed their position would be to deny any liability for loss.

In Mobiqa Ltd v Trinity Mobile Ltd the defendant's refusal to mediate was not unreasonable. The Defendant argued that mediation should take place once *"the parties' expert evidence had been exchanged, so it could be seen whether in fact the Claimant had any case."* Contrast this, however, with PGF II SA v OMFS Company 1 Ltd: *"Experience suggests that many disputes, are resolved before all material necessary for a trial is available. Either parties know or are prepared to assume that certain facts will be established . The rationale behind the Halsey decision is the saving of costs and this is achieved (or at least attempted) by the parties being prepared to compromise without necessarily having as complete a picture of the other parties' case as would be available at trial."*

There may well be circumstances in which a lack of information may justify refusal of ADR at a particular point in time, but a simple rejection of an offer of ADR may well lead to costs risk. The refusing party is better off responding with proposals to rectify the situation, for example providing details of evidence required, an explanation of its relevance to ADR, a timeframe for obtaining evidence and a window for ADR thereafter. Parties should not, however, expect full evidence such as would be available at trial and certainly the fact full disclosure has not taken place does not appear to be a good reason to refuse ADR. The question is whether key evidence needed to engage in meaningful ADR is absent, and if so how can this be rectified in order to permit ADR.

<u>Distrust between the parties</u>

Parties in litigation often dislike each other, but this is not good reason to refuse ADR. In Garritt-Critchley v Ronnan it was argued that a key factor in the decision not to mediate was *".. that there was a considerable dislike and mistrust between the parties, "* The court said: *"And in any event it is precisely where there may be distrust or emotion between the parties, which it might be thought is pushing them down the road to an expensive trial, where the skills of a mediator come in most usefully. They are well trained to diffuse emotion, feelings of distrust and other matters in order that the parties can see their way to a commercial settlement. So I consider that that is a reason which does not have any real foundation either."*

<u>Offering ADR as a tactic</u>

It is advisable to offer ADR and to accept offers to engage in ADR in most cases. This is because the courts are seeking to incentivise parties to engage in ADR. Of course, a party who makes an offer of ADR will be expected to follow it through. One that makes a tactical offer and then withdraws it is equally at risk of sanction, unless they can put forward a strong justification for doing so.

Where an offer is properly set out, the courts are in any event unlikely to conclude it is tactical. In *PGF*, the court considered whether the offer to mediate was merely tactical but found, on the contrary that it was: *"a serious and carefully formulated written invitation"* and was *"couched in such detailed and sensible terms that it could not reasonably have been regarded as a mere tactic"*.

Sanctions imposed by the courts for failing to engage in ADR

The following cases, also referred to above, are examples provide examples of the costs sanctions imposed for failure to engage in ADR:

<u>PGF II SA v OMFS Company 1 Ltd</u>

The usual Part 36 rule was amended and the defendant was disallowed its costs from the expiry of its Part 36 offer to the date of settlement (approximately 12 months and £250,000 costs).

<u>Lynn v Borneos LLP t/a Borneo Linnels</u>

The successful party's costs were reduced by 40%. The court took into account the fact that although it could not be said there would be no value in going to mediation there was not a high possibility that a settlement would have been achieved.

<u>Garritt-Critchley and Others v Ronnan and Solarpower PV Limited</u>

The unsuccessful defendant was ordered to pay the claimant's costs on the indemnity basis.

<u>Laporte & Anor v The Commissioner of Police of the Metropolis</u>

The defendant's costs were reduced by 33%, notwithstanding he was successful on every substantive issue.

<u>Rana v Tears of Sutton Bridge</u>

The successful defendant's costs were reduced by 40%.

<u>Reid v Buckinghamshire Healthcare NHS Trust</u>

The paying party was ordered to pay indemnity costs on the detailed assessment costs from the period after the receiving party's offer to mediate.

Bristow v The Princess Alexander Hospital NHS Trust & Ors

The paying party was ordered to pay indemnity costs on the whole of the detailed assessment costs.

In this case the defendant failed to attend an agreed mediation. This was described by the court as serious misconduct. It was also sufficient to entitle the court to dismiss the application for security for costs.

The Without Prejudice Save as to Costs Rule

It is well known that refusal to mediate can lead to costs penalties. What may be less understood is when the parties can draw this to the attention of the Court.

In R (on the application of Wildbur) v Ministry of Defence [2016] EWHC 821 (Admin), the court found that even the fact of a failure to reply to an offer of mediation (if there was such a failure) was protected by the without prejudice rule.

There are various circumstances where evidence of without prejudice communications can be admitted, such as where the issue is whether a concluded settlement has been reached, or where the fact of negotiations taking place is needed to explain a party's delay.

In the case of Wildbur the claimant was seeking judicial review of the MoD's decision on a "service complaint" he had lodged after he was made redundant. In granting permission for judicial review, the judge encouraged the parties to try to settle the matter, including by the use of mediation.

The claimant proposed mediation. The MoD then wrote proposing a without prejudice meeting. A consent order was made staying directions for a period to allow the parties "to undertake alternative dispute resolution".

A without prejudice meeting took place but was unsuccessful and the case continued. The MoD objected to two paragraphs of the claimant's reply to the MoJ's defence. These passages stated that the MoD had "refused mediation", attending only an "informal meeting" .

The judge ordered the passages to be struck out on the basis that they had disclosed the content of Without prejudice communications. The judge found that the without prejudice rule applied to a failure to reply to an offer as much as to an actual reply. This principle was not limited to specific offers of settlement; it applied equally to the fact of an offer of settlement negotiations.

In many cases, a party who proposes mediation will want to be able to point that out, and any refusal or failure to respond on the part of its opponent, once the court comes to consider the issue of costs, after the main issues have been determined, but not before. That is perfectly acceptable if the correspondence has been marked "without prejudice save as to costs." Otherwise it won't be possible to refer to it.

Refusal to mediate in costs disputes

In relation to detailed assessment of costs, the Part 36 rules apply and there is also an incentive to use ADR.

The High Court sent a strong signal on the financial penalties of refusing to mediate in costs proceedings in two judgments against the NHS Litigation Authority. This applies to unsuccessful parties and not just successful parties being deprived of their costs.

In Reid v Buckinghamshire Healthcare NHS Trust, Master O'Hare awarded the claimant its costs on the indemnity basis from three days after the Claimant's solicitors had made an offer of alternative dispute resolution.

The Master said the defendant's failure to mediate had been 'unreasonable', and noted that it took the defendant 'six weeks' to reply to the offer, declining to mediate.

In another case, Bristow, the court went further, ordering all costs to be paid on the indemnity basis, from the date that work commenced rather than from the date of the offer to mediate.

The Claimant's solicitor said the Reid case 'is not a warning, it's a declaration of war against any party that refuses to engage in ADR.'

He added: 'We have known since Halsey that successful parties who refuse to engage in ADR will only recover a fraction of their costs. But [Reid] is the first case in which an unsuccessful party has been punished...

'The court could not be clearer that there was no good reason for refusing to engage in ADR in costs cases. Parties who refuse, will face sanctions.'

Essentially the Court was willing to punish the NHS LA where it had not taken up offers to mediate in costs disputes". Rightly or wrongly the message is "mediate or else"!

Practice Points – Ways to offer ADR or refuse it

In general terms the issue of whether or not to engage in ADR may arise because:

1. You offer ADR; or

2. The other party instigates ADR: or

3. the court encourages the parties to mediate;

If you instigate the proposal to engage in ADR, it is probably best not to raise any reference to the CPR or the cases in the first instance. An amicable decision, made jointly in a case discussion on the basis that ADR may well settle the case, is undoubtedly the best foundation.

If, however, you meet with a refusal, resistance or a "perhaps, but not now" response you may wish to refer to the case law to persuade the other party to reconsider and/or the court to make a direction to encourage and facilitate ADR. Such persuasion will normally involve a number of steps:

1. An unambiguous written offer to undertake ADR, noting that previous discussions have not reached agreement on this point,

citing the particular reasons why the case is appropriate for ADR and why now is a suitable time. Alternatively, if evidence is required before ADR, setting out the steps you propose in order to secure this and the proposed date for ADR

2. A review of the reasons given for any refusal:

    (a) If detailed written reasons for a refusal are not given, call for them, referring to *PGF* which clearly articulates the requirement for contemporaneous written reasons, and reserve the right to refer to the correspondence when costs fall to be considered. It is important to make the correspondence explicitly "without prejudice save as to costs" as if it is marked only "without prejudice" there is authority for the proposition that it cannot be referred to.

    (b) If detailed written reasons for a refusal are stated, these should be considered and compared with the reasons previously put before the courts. If the reasons are not good ones in light of the authorities, set out why this is so and invite reconsideration of the offer. Again reserve the right to refer to the correspondence when costs fall to be considered.

    (c) If no agreement to engage in ADR is forthcoming and you remain of the view that the reasons said to justify refusal are insufficient, the issue can be referred to the court next time you are before it.

    (d) If there is no response at all to the offer, write again, and reiterate that silence in the face of an offer to mediate will usually amount to an unreasonable refusal which should sound in costs.

If the opposing party or the court instigates the proposal to mediate and your client, on advice, wishes to reject the proposal, it will be necessary to draft and send written reasons justifying the refusal, which reasons must be consistent with *Halsey*, *PGF* and the recent cases. Where you seek to rely on reasons which are similar to those outlined above, which have previously been rejected by the court, it will be necessary to establish why the stated reasons are sufficient and distinguishable from those that have been rejected.

<u>Is a refusal to engage in ADR always going to result in sanctions?</u>

There were a number of post-*Halsey* decisions where a refusal to engage in ADR was found to be reasonable.

In Society Internationale de Telecommunications Aeronautiques S.C. v Wyatt & Co (UK) Limited the court found that it was reasonable for a Part 20 Defendant to refuse to participate in a mediation offered by the Claimant shortly before the trial of the Part 20 claim.

In S v Chapman a Defendant was found to be entitled to await the outcome of its application to strike out before deciding whether or not it was necessary or advantageous to enter into mediation.

What about the "Perhaps we will engage in ADR, but not now" delaying response? In Mobiqa Ltd v Trinity Mobile the defendant was found to be justified in arguing expert evidence should first be exchanged, though this should be read with the important caveat in PGF II SA v OMFS Company 1 Ltd, that parties cannot expect to have as complete a picture of the other party's case as they would at trial. Any proposals to defer on the basis that further evidence is needed should be limited to key evidence, should explain what it is and why it is of such importance to ADR, and should set out a timetable for obtaining the evidence and proceed with ADR at a later date. A bare refusal on this basis, however reasoned, is unlikely to be met with much sympathy by the Court.

In R (Royal Free London NHS Foundation Trust) v Secretary of State for the Home Department it was held that an offer to mediate which is made subject to an unreasonable pre condition will be disregarded.

It would not be unreasonable to engage in an exchange in relation to the form of ADR. For example, a proposal for a JSM may be met with a counter proposal for mediation, with reasons. However, considering the encouragement towards ADR, parties should not allow the form of dispute resolution to become a sticking point as this risks sanction from the Court. A tactical advantage can be gained by offering ADR at the outset, particularly if faced with an uncooperative or unresponsive opponent, as a failure to respond can act as an insurance policy in the event that your side loses the case.

In our view there is an increasing use of offers to mediate as a tactic and so parties should always respond to an invitation to mediate with an acceptance or fully argued reasons as to why it is not appropriate at that stage or at all. In practice, it is hard to justify a blanket refusal.

Summary

- There are few circumstances where a refusal to mediate is reasonable even in a clear cut case. The Courts have moved on since Halsey.

- If you don't want to mediate then make sure the reasons are set out and you put forward a plan to get ready to mediate.

- An offer to mediate can work to a party's tactical advantage if the other party refuses or ignores the request.

- An offer to mediate should be made "without prejudice save as to costs" so that it can be relied upon in Court.

CHAPTER TWELVE
UNDER-SETTLEMENT RISK

A key role of the personal injury lawyer is to value the claim and negotiate a settlement. Most cases settle so as to avoid the uncertainty and expense of going to trial, but valuation is not a perfect science. It is a question of assessing the various heads of loss and arriving at value range that a judge is likely to award at trial and at a figure that the claimant is willing to accept and the defendant to pay.

In some cases, because of the inexperience and or negligence of the law firm or claims company a claim may have been settled at a value that is too low. In such a case, the victim of the under settlement may well make a claim against their legal advisers. There has been a noticeable increase in "cannibalistic" professional negligence claims.

The first element in a valuation is pain and suffering and loss of amenity, or 'general damages'. The Judicial College guidelines and previous cases help with this process, and as a general rule the seriousness of the initial injury and the extend of any future disability are the most important factors, but pain and disability are difficult to measure objectively and no two cases will be the same. Other important variables include the amount of overlap between multiple injuries, the claimant's age and personal circumstances, so for instance an amputated little finger will be a devastating injury to a concert pianist and a facial scar may destroy the earnings potential of a model.

In addition to compensation for the injuries themselves, there will usually be a claim for other losses and expenses, or "special damages". The purpose of personal injury damages is to put the injured person back into the position they would have been if the accident had not happened, so far as it is possible for money to do this. So there will often be a claim for loss of earnings whilst the injured person is unable to work and perhaps an ongoing loss where they return to work but in a less well paid capacity or if they need to retrain for alternative work.

There may be a compensation claim for loss of pension, loss of profit from a self-employed business, loss of earnings capacity or loss of a vocation. In serious injury cases there will often be claims for future care and support: adaptations to the home, workplace or car, care and support or case management, future surgery or other medical treatment, aids and equipment. Future loss claims can become very complex, with legal and medical arguments about what is needed, how long for, how much it should cost and how it should be funded. In less serious cases there will still often be a claim for care, gardening, DIY, motoring, medical and other expenses.

It can be seen from the above that any a single settlement figure is made up of many components and each of these components will be calculated on the basis of a number of pieces of evidence. While this may seem self evident, reflecting on the large number of factors at play demonstrates the way in which under-settlements may come about.

When additional factors such as liability disputes, contributory negligence, medical questions of causation, risk of future deterioration or a change in circumstances are considered the impossibility of arriving at a ' correct ' figure in most cases becomes clear.

The valuation of loss is only one part of the equation. Unless liability is admitted in full then an allowance will have to be made for the litigation risk – the chance of losing the case entirely or of losing part of the claim for 'contributory negligence'.

Does this mean that litigators should not engage in ADR until all avenues have been investigated and evidence is complete? In our view the answer is no, and the previous chapter demonstrates that the courts will not be sympathetic to such an approach.

Full and final settlement

Barring provisional damages or variable periodical payments, which are rare, all settlements are full and final. This may be obvious to professional litigators, but clients may not fully realise what it means to them. Clear advice is key here, as some clients may be surprised to know that even a serious (but perhaps unlikely) deterioration in their condition would not permit them to re-open their case.

Your case is only as good as your evidence

However, the determination of any case, and also any settlement, must be evidence based. A claimant needs to be able to prove losses, on a balance of probabilities. So, the claimant, with assistance from his solicitor, has to prove the value of the claim by expert and other evidence. A claimant may believe that a back condition is wholly attributable to an accident, but if their expert takes a different view (for example that there was no more than an acceleration) then the expert's opinion can be expected to prevail at trial. A self employed claimant who is a poor book keeper may have to accept he is only likely to record on the basis of recorded earnings, even if he believes he may have had higher takings.

This applies equally to trial as to ADR. If the evidence does not turn out as the claimant hoped, then settlement on the available evidence is not under settlement, but a prudent course. Indeed where evidence is not developing in accordance with expectations, a party may consider engaging ADR before they have to show their hand, for example when disclosure or other evidence is due to be provided to their opponent.

Asking the right questions, pursuing the right investigations

Arriving at a reasonable settlement range is a combination of assessing known losses and ruling out other potential heads of loss. Any practitioner should explore with their client the broadest possible range of losses arriving from an accident, to rule out lines of enquiry and identify areas which need further exploration. They then need to engage with their client throughout investigations to explore possible sources of evidence.

Proportionate investigations are reasonable

So long as the client understands that the approach is being taken, it is legitimate for a practitioner to constrain their investigations in a way that is proportionate. Indeed, as soon as the court begins to case manage, proportionality will become mandatory.

Since funding rules in personal injury claims were reformed in 2013 and the introduction of costs budgeting, proportionality has become an increasingly important aspect of client care for claimant's representative. Success fees, budget overruns and ATE may all be the claimant's liability, and so proportionality of investigations ensures a claimant obtains the maximum proportion of the damages award.

What is proportionate? Needless to say that depends on the value of the claim, but also on the value of the evidence being pursued so that there is no general rule. Different clients may take a different view as to the level of investigation that they wish to pursue. What's important is that avenues of investigation are considered proactively, costs and benefits explained to clients and consensus reached as to the investigation to be undertaken.

Impact of risk on settlements

There are a range of risks in litigation, and it does not amount to under settlement to arrive at an outcome which takes these into account. A liability disputed claim may have an all or nothing outcome if taken to trial– in those circumstances both parties may be better served by the certainty of compromise somewhere between these extremes.

To give a practical example, a claimant will mobility problems following an accident may have a claim in relation to general damages, single story accommodation and gratuitous care from their partner. If they win at trial, they will get damages for all three. If they lose they will get none. On the other hand, compromising at 50% may be enough for them to move to a bungalow, where they will continue to be supported by their partner. The couple will not have the same financial benefit, but they can afford the home they need.

Risk also applies in relation to evidence and quantum. A further report or other evidential step may support a party's case, or may damage it, and as we have stated above there is a range of possible assessments of quantum in all injury cases.

Further risk arises when it comes to costs. As we have seen a refusal to engage in ADR or to accept a good Part 36 offer may create a risk to costs recovery or of an adverse costs order.

It's the client's claim

It is always important to remember as a practitioner that the claim is your client's and they will have a view on how they wish it to be run. The practitioner's job is to advise on the legal position, options and risk. May clients may prefer to settle for less now than to go through lengthy legal proceedings, even where the outcome may be financially better for them. That is a legitimate decision the client to make, and one that should be respected by practitioners. If a client decides to accept a lower offer, or to work towards an earlier settlement even if this may mean a less good deal than could otherwise be available, it is not for their advisor to get in the way of that.

Why are cases under-settled?

None of the observations above should come as any surprise to readers, so why are claims still under-settled in some cases?

The most common problems are where the lawyer lacks the necessary skill or expertise to value and negotiate the case properly, or where the pressure of time and fees leads to short cuts being made. Increasingly, there is pressure in the personal injury claims industry to reduce costs, with the introduction of fixed fees. This can mean junior or unqualified case handlers running claims, and being required to run them quickly and at minimal cost. In those circumstances, mistakes can easily be made.

Another development is that very many personal injury claims are handled by claims management companies, either initially or throughout. Claims management companies are not regulated in the same way as lawyers and their staff are not qualified to litigate. Their business models are often geared towards claims processing rather than resolving difficult legal issues, and they may not be able to provide the quality of service necessary for personal injury clients. This may mean that the important questions mentioned above are missed, or that claims which do not fit a standard model are not given the attention they need in order to be properly valued.

A claim can be under-settled if solicitor representative makes mistakes or is negligent during the process of pleading the claim, gathering evidence and conducting negotiations with the other parties involved. Some examples of situations where something could go wrong with a personal injury claim, causing it to be under-settled include:

- Failure to get appropriate medical evidence of injuries. This can include cases where no medical report was commissioned, or where the doctor examining did not have sufficient medical knowledge to undertake a proper assessment or to provide a prognosis.

- Failure to negotiate effectively with the party responsible for causing the accident. For example, solicitors may accept the first offer put forward by an insurer for their client's compensation, without bothering to contact their client to see if they are happy with this figure, or to put forward an alternate figure. The figure may be within a pre- authorized settlement range, agreed with the client, but a brief further negotiation could still lead to a better deal.

- Failure to consider all of the financial losses in a claim. Common mistakes include failure to fully recover loss of earnings, loss of overtime and any missed pension contributions, or failure to consider a claim for the time and trouble spent by family and friends who provided care following an accident.

- Firms of solicitors who rely on inexperienced junior members of staff to run personal injury compensation claims. This can lead to mistakes being made on files and problems such as missed deadlines or poor communication between solicitor and client and can in some circumstances, result in a claim being under-settled.

<u>All types of Personal Injury claims can be affected by under-settling</u>

The level of under-settling in a particular claim can also vary from a few hundred pounds to tens or hundreds of thousands in cases involving serious injuries, or injuries with lengthy recovery periods or potential complications.

Claims relating to under-settlement

Until recently, it was relatively difficult to make a professional negligence claim against a solicitor for under-settling a claim, as the courts were reluctant to award the claimant their legal costs. This meant that any claim that was brought would have to be funded by their claimant out of their own pocket, making it too expensive for all but a handful of potential claimants to take their cases to court.

However, following an increase in reports of under-settling in personal injury claims, professional negligence solicitors, are now willing and able to take on these claims. This is often on the basis that a percentage of the money recovered in the event of a successful claim will be used to pay the legal fees of your professional negligence solicitor.

In Dixon v Clement Jones Solicitors [2004] EWCA Civ 1005 Lord Justice Rix said:

> *"There is no requirement in such a loss of a chance case to fight out a trial within a trial, indeed the authorities show as a whole that that is what should be avoided. It is the prospects and not the hypothetical decision in the lost trial that have to be investigated. ….*
> *The test is not to find what the original decision of the underlying litigation would have been as if that litigation had been fought out, but to assess what the prospects were."*

An example of an under settled case which ended up being litigated again against the solicitors as a professional negligence claim was Raleys Solicitors v Barnaby [2014] EWCA Civ 686 (21 May 2014)

The claimant had been employed as a miner and had used vibratory tools. This had led to him developing vibration white finger, or VWF, and Hand Arm Vibration Syndrome, HAVS.

Raleys Solicitors were appointed to pursue a personal injury claim on his behalf. However, when his injury claim settled it only included compensation for the injury itself, together with a further sum for "handicap on the labour market". He had also indicated an intention to make a claim for services which were required as a consequence of his disability. However, he abandoned his services claim following advice by Raleys.. On 6 December 2002 he agreed to settle his claim for a total of £10,822.01 plus interest. He later commenced proceedings against Raleys for professional negligence in relation to their advice.

On 25 July 2013 in Leeds County Court His Honour Judge Gosnell (the Judge) found negligence on the part of Raleys and awarded Mr Barnaby damages of £5,925 on the basis of the loss of a chance of further recovery from the Scheme as to which he would have had a seventy five per cent prospect of success. On appeal, Raleys contend that the judge was wrong to find a causal connection between the (now) admitted negligence and the failure of the services claim. Raleys alone advised over 12,000 coal miners on VWF claims against the Scheme. Raleys sought to raise questions over Mr Barnaby's honesty in the original claim, alleging that he had never had vibration white finger. They sought to argue that the claimant abandoned his claim for services because he knew he had no real need for services not because he was negligently advised.

The Court of Appeal rejected Raley's points. The judge commented that "Whilst it is true that Mr Barnaby was "a poor historian and an unimpressive witness", the attack on his honesty, which was sustained and unequivocal, seems to me to have been misjudged. One has to keep in mind that his original claim was in relation to the Scheme and was not one made in the course of conventional civil litigation".

...I am entirely satisfied that the Judge correctly assessed the reality behind this litigation. Solicitors who had encouraged and certainly not discouraged the presentation of a services claim are now seeking to characterise it as misconceived on the basis of material which was irrelevant to it and in the face of evidence which would probably have led to its success – or at least the quantified prospect of success – but for the intervention of negligent advice which caused Mr Barnaby to abandon it in circumstances in which neither he nor anyone else would otherwise have abandoned it. There would have been no credible reason for him to have done so."

In other similar cases, claims have succeeded where solicitors failed to ask the right questions to reveal a services claim, or advise that such a claim may be available.

It is estimated that 170,000 injury claims were brought under the Government's Miners Compensation scheme. Over 100,000 of those claims would have attracted compensation for "services". However, it is thought that less than half actually included a "services" award. It is clear that this scheme alone could give rise to numerous further under-settlement claims. If similar trends are found in areas of the wider personal injury claims arena then a very high volume of potential claims exist.

Practitioners who prepare properly for ADR, and understand and are able to convey to their clients the pros and cons of ADR as well as of any settlement are likely to significantly reduce their exposure to such claims.

Summary

- There is a tension between the requirement to mediate and the risk that a case may be under settled if the case is not ready or properly prepared.

- Under settlement cases are assessed on the basis of a loss of chance.

- Practitioners should explain the pros and cons of the ADR process to the client and settlement recommendations in order to minimise the risk of claims.

CHAPTER THIRTEEN
RE-OPENING SETTLEMENTS

When parties are negotiating a settlement in a personal injury case, how can they be sure that they are settling at the right level and that the Claimant is telling the truth? This type of situation is not uncommon, for example, on commencement of court proceedings or prior to trial when insurers carry out further investigations and find new evidence or take an alternative view on a case seek to resile from an earlier admission of liability.

What if the case has been settled? Can a settlement be challenged at a later date if it is found that the settlement was incorrect, or the claim was originally fraudulent, exaggerated or based on misrepresentations? As Lord Toulson said in Hayward v Zurich "Bogus or fraudulently inflated personal injury claims are not new. One of the great advocates of the 20th century, Sir Patrick Hastings, recounted vividly in his memoirs, "Cases in Court" (William Heinemann Ltd, 1949, pp 4 to 20), how as a young barrister before World War 1 he built up a practice defending insurance companies against such claims. Now as then, they present a serious problem. Personal injury claims usually fall to be met by insurers and the ultimate cost is borne by other policy holders through increased premiums.

Insurers may often have grounds for suspicion about a claim but lack the hard evidence necessary to prove fraud. To pursue an allegation of fraud without strong evidence is risky. If in such circumstances insurers settle a claim, not in the belief that it is bona fide but in the belief that it is likely to succeed, and if afterwards they discover evidence which proves that the claim was fraudulent, can they bring proceedings to set aside the agreement and recover damages for deceit? In this case the judge at first instance said yes, but the Court of Appeal said no, because in such circumstances the insurers were not deceived. The question of which court gave the right answer is important, both for insurers and for those who advise personal injury claimants."

In a Norcross v Georgallides 2015 a party argued that he had been induced by fraudulent representation to enter into a settlement agreement. It was held that it was inherently unlikely that the Claimant would have relied on the representations in the evidence presented in the case, because it was unlikely that he believed the evidence to be true.

The Court has subsequently looked into the issue in great detail in Hayward v Zurich, now the leading case on the subject

Hayward v Zurich

The leading personal injury case on the subject, is Hayward v Zurich, in which the defendants sought to re-open a personal injury settlement. The Claimant had injured his back in an accident at work and pleaded a claim of over £400,000. The Defendant suspected fraud and produced surveillance in support. The parties agreed to settle his claim upon payment of £134,973. Two years later his neighbours told his employers that he had completely recovered from the injury at least 6 months before the settlement was reached.

The Defendant's insurers went back to Court to argue that the Claimant should repay the settlement money on the basis of deceit and fraudulent misrepresentation. The issue was whether, having settled in the knowledge the case might be fraudulent, at a level which presumably took into account that risk, the insurers could then allege inducement by misrepresentation or deceit. The Court of Appeal thought not – the insurers did understand the nature of the claim they were settling and elected to compromise. The Supreme Court however set aside the settlement agreement, stating the issue was whether the Defendant had been influenced by deliberate exaggeration – if so then the misrepresentation had induced the settlement at the level agreed.

More generally, it could be said that the decision reflects the court's unwillingness to tolerate fraud within litigation, even where it is only proved following settlement.

Summary

- A settlement can be unravelled in cases where fraud is later discovered but it is not straightforward.

- In mediation the parties usually agree that the mediator will not give evidence about the mediation and so it will be difficult to prove the motivations behind the settlement.

- The question is likely to turn upon whether a party was deceived during the course of the ADR process.

- Parties wishing to re-open a settlement will have to pierce the "without prejudice" veil, which is not straightforward, particularly in relation to a mediation where the parties have agreed confidentiality applies and have agreed that the mediator will not be compelled to give evidence.

CHAPTER FOURTEEN
THE FUTURE: ODR – OH,
BRAVE NEW LITIGATION WORLD
THAT HAS SUCH ADR PEOPLE IN IT!

With continuing downwards pressure on costs and increases in Court fees, commoditization and summary online procedures, ADR is only likely to increase. Following Briggs LJ's final report on the Civil Courts Structure, published in July 2016, ADR is likely to play an increasing role in personal injury cases in the future. He did not rule out including personal injury claims in the Online "Solutions" Court, as recommended by the Civil Justice Council. ADR will be a key part of the Online Court at stage 2.

The stage 1 process of the Online Court is designed to give both parties that level of information about each other's case, the absence of which is often an impediment to successful pre-issue ADR. Sophisticated pre-action protocols are designed to fill that gap in litigation normally conducted between represented parties, but stage 1 triage is likely to replace that in cases of the type suitable for the Online Court. Briggs LJ adds that he does not regard the erection of a pre-action protocol procedure as at all suitable to the Online Court. At the most it might recommend a simple exchange of correspondence. Briggs LJ regards ADR as being an essential element in a new Court designed for navigation by litigants without lawyers, or lawyers on limited retainers with limited costs recovery.

Briggs LJ says that there has been no significant appetite for the inclusion of PI claims (including those based on clinical negligence), at least those which are, or will remain in, the Fast Track, with its fixed recoverable costs and streamlined Portal for their litigation.

Briggs LJ refers in his report to the government proposal, announced in the 2015 Autumn Statement, to raise the threshold for personal injury cases in the Small Claims Track (and therefore to remove significant costs shifting), so as to include claims between £1,000 and £5,000. The anticipated MoJ consultation on this proposal has yet to be published and it is unclear now whether it will proceed. If the small claims threshold was raised, then it would be over-simplistic to assume that the claims thereby downgraded to the Small Claims Track should simply fall into the Online Court, as it were by default. Briggs LJ suggests that the RTA Portal which has already expanded beyond its original scope, could expand further.

In Briggs LJ's view the forum should be a matter for the choice of PI claimants. If they were otherwise forced into the Small Claims Track and thereby deprived of legal representation, then he cannot see why they should be excluded from the benefits with which the Online Court is (or could be) designed to provide them. But if the PI stakeholders can re-construct a new economic model which keeps such claims in the RTA Portal, and if that route would be incompatible with the Online Court (which does not necessarily follow for disputed claims) then again, the decision should lie with the claimants.

Now that the proposals to increase the small claims limit for personal injury claims is back on the agenda, the objective seems to be to save cost and remove lawyers from the process at the lower end of the system. We wonder whether this will lead to increased use of ADR for these claims.

Current government policy in relation to court fees is to increase them to make the system self-sufficient. The effect of the April 2014 fee increases was to cause only a temporary fall in Fast Track claims, which have since recovered. A long term rising trend in small claims has continued (there having been no fee increases in that track), but Fast track claims show no clear pattern of growth or decline. By contrast, the fall in Multi-track claims has continued thereafter, and most commentators suggest that this is indeed caused, at least in substantial part, by the much steeper fee increases attributable to those claims than to the Fast Track. It may therefore reasonably be concluded that the current fee policy does discourage access to the civil courts for claims where the amount claimed exceeds £25,000. It is widely believed within the same community that the recent sharp rises in issue fees for Multi-track civil claims has led to an increase in mediation before the issue of proceedings. These are cases which might well previously have mediated after issue, so the increased fees do not necessarily increase the proportion of underlying disputes that go to mediation. Nor does the increase in pre-issue ADR mean that these cases necessarily settle any earlier down the process of incurring disproportionate costs. This is because more of the costs are also now incurred pre-issue, for example by detailed exchanges of pre-action correspondence between solicitors, sometimes including draft statements of case, witness statements and even experts' reports.

In relation to higher value claims, Briggs LJ noted that there appears to be a particular shortfall in the potential penetration of mediation in relation to personal injuries and clinical negligence claims. Feedback from the International Mediation Institute suggests that this particular shortfall is not a consequence of the underlying nature of those types of dispute, because personal injury and clinical negligence claims are widely and successfully mediated in other countries.

Since there is a general consensus that it is usually better for parties to civil litigation to be empowered to settle their own disputes, than to have them determined in court, Briggs LJ considers that, both within and beyond the confines of the proposed Online Court, steps ought actively to be taken to re-establish or replace the discontinued national mediation helpline and after hours mediation services on a much broader basis than is currently represented by the Small Claims Mediation service. Currently the Small Claims mediation service excludes personal injury claims from its remit. He recommended re-establishing a court-based out of hours private mediation service in County Court hearing centres prepared to participate, along the lines of the service which existed prior to the establishment and then termination of the National Mediation Helpline.

There is an appetite within the NHSLA to expand its use of ADR. The minutes of the NHSLA's AGM in 2016 indicate that the NHSLA sees mediation as showing promising signs of helping them in resolving claims fairly and promptly in appropriate cases. They consider that mediation enables them to obtain good value for the NHS and also enables them to generate positive outcome for both patients and the service on claims. This comes at a time when the cost of claims and damages has increased dramatically.

It states that:

> *"The NHS LA continues to have an important role in ensuring that cases where there has been no negligence or where there is an important point of principle to be tested are contested appropriately. We significantly increased the number of cases we took to trial this year by 45% in total whilst maintaining a success rate of 60%..."*

> *"We recognise that we share a number of common aims with firms who act for claimants. In particular it is a core aim of the NHSLA to resolve claims promptly and fairly, to get to the right answer as soon as possible and to deliver compensation swiftly where it is due. Although this is not always straightforward as even where there is evidence of failings in care, it is necessary to obtain medical evidence to establish whether that led to the injury, or severity of injury, complained of. The consequences of what happened and the cost of the consequences can often be as much a source of dispute as whether or not mistakes were made. However, it is an ambition of ours to avoid the need for expensive litigation and find other ways to resolve claims for compensation which do not involve court proceedings. This is an aim which we share, and have started to address, with the claimant legal community"*

The report states that they aim to progress further this through the use of mediation - *"A successful pilot was undertaken within the year demonstrating how powerful meditation can represent in clinical negligence disputes. The purpose of the pilot was to give mediation a renewed impetus and to examine the barriers to its use. A number of fatal and elderly care claims were selected as being particularly suitable for mediation but this was by no means the only area on which we focussed our efforts with mediation continuing to be offered on all suitable claims. The pilot clearly demonstrated the benefits and a procurement will be undertaken for a mediation service in the coming year."*

The MPS noted the plans to extend the mediation pilot and procuring for providers and asked whether they would be going to extend the category of cases. The response was interesting in that the NHSLA pilot focused on fatal and elderly care because in its view those cases were particularly susceptible to mediation as an approach and often involve issues that involve the wider family. They will be extending the service to all suitable cases and saw the pilot as an opportunity to given an impetus to their aim to see greater take-up of mediation across the clinical portfolio.

Part of the NHSLA pilot process was to ensure that all of their senior claims senior staff had undertaken mediation training so they were up to speed on the latest models for mediation.

They recognised that mediation requires different skills. Some lawyers may have tried mediation over 10 years ago and found that the process was akin to a trial in terms of preparation. Nowadays however there is a different model and one of the things they learnt from the pilot is that it was important to "up-skill" their lawyers and own staff to ensure they were fully versed in how mediations can work, how we get the best of out of them and also which cases are most suitable.

The government has woken up to the issue of costs deriving from clinical negligence claims and the direction of travel involves more ADR, linked in with transparency about standards. So, for example, the government has announced that it will release new ratings for maternity wards across England to allow prospective parents to compare and contrast services in NHS hospitals, as part of a drive to reduce instances of stillbirth and brain injuries during labour. The Health Secretary also unveil proposals to allow the NHS to offer compensation automatically to parents of babies left stillborn or brain-damaged because of poor care. The health secretary wants parents of children starved of oxygen at birth no longer to have to wait of about 11 years for compensation and to cut down on unnecessary legal costs.

An independent rapid resolution and redress scheme will be set up to investigate deaths in childbirth, which would quickly decide whether compensation should be paid. This comes as figures showed that the cost of settling claims with parents whose children are damaged at birth has reached more than £0.5bn. The NHS as a whole pays out more than £1bn a year in negligence compensation, and reducing that cost is seen a key way of mitigating the financial crisis facing the service. The Health secretary said he hoped to end the culture where going to court was an automatic "first step" and instead foster a culture of transparency so the NHS can learn from its mistakes.

Under the plans, claims by parents who believe medical errors have caused severe damage to their children, such as cerebral palsy or brain damage, would be assessed by investigators working independently of the NHS trust. The investigators would quiz NHS staff and parents and look at medical records. Their findings would be presented to a panel of legal and medical experts who would decide whether any compensation is warranted and arrange for payments to be made to the family. The government hopes the scheme, which would assess about 500 cases a year, will help dismantle what it sees as a "litigation culture." Data from the NHS Litigation Authority shows the compensation bill to the NHS for errors around the time of birth is rising, reaching £509.3m in 2015/16 – up from £393.2m in 2014/15. A spokeswoman for the Department of Health said the plan, which will be the subject of a con-sultation, will not be binding and would let them bring their own legal case against the trust if they were unhappy with the outcome.

The new maternity ward ratings follow the creation of similar schemes to help patients and families compare the quality of cancer and demen-tia care. We anticipate that other ADR schemes will be set up to deal with clinical negligence claims if this is successful.

From the above, we can see that ADR and in particular mediation is a key theme within both court reform plans and the strategy of one of the largest injury claim defendants, the NHS LA. Insurers and other defen-dants are increasingly exploring the opportunities ADR offers. There is a drive to make dispute resolution 'self service' in some areas, excluding legal practitioners from the process or designing a process within which practitioners will provide unbundles services. There can be little doubt that if (or, we suspect, when) these changes do come it will mean a real shift in the litigation services market. However, for ADR to work there has to be a benchmark, and this, for the present, is likely to continue to be set by the courts, through litigation. Lawyers will continue to have a role both in those cases which do litigate and in advising clients on how to apply decisions arrives at through litigation to resolve disputes.

What is certain is that lawyers, claims handlers, and even litigants of the future will need a different attitude to ADR – as we observed at the outset, in the future we may see the "A" taken out of ADR, as the methods of dispute resolution discussed in this book become the norm.

MORE BOOKS BY
LAW BRIEF PUBLISHING

'A Practical Guide to Holiday Sickness Claims' by Andrew Mckie & Ian Skeate
'Ellis and Kevan on Credit Hire, 5ᵗʰ Edition' by Aidan Ellis & Tim Kevan
'RTA Allegations of Fraud in a Post-Jackson Era: The Handbook, 2ⁿᵈ Edition' by Andrew Mckie
'RTA Personal Injury Claims: A Practical Guide Post-Jackson' by Andrew Mckie
'A Practical Guide to Personal Injuries in Sport' by Adam Walker & Patricia Leonard
'A Practical Approach to Clinical Negligence Post-Jackson' by Geoffrey Simpson-Scott
'A Practical Guide to Costs in Personal Injury Cases' by Matthew Hoe
'Occupiers, Highways and Defective Premises Claims: A Practical Guide Post-Jackson' by Andrew Mckie
'Employers' Liability Claims: A Practical Guide Post-Jackson' by Andrew Mckie
'A Practical Guide to Subtle Brain Injury Claims' by Pankaj Madan
'Baby Steps: A Guide to Maternity Leave and Maternity Pay' by Leah Waller
'The Queen's Counsel Lawyer's Omnibus: 20 Years of Cartoons from the Times 1993-2013' by Alex Steuart Williams

These books and more are available to order online direct from the publisher at www.lawbriefpublishing.com, where you can also read free sample chapters. For any queries, contact us on 0844 587 2383 or mail@lawbriefpublishing.com.

Our books are also usually in stock at www.amazon.co.uk with free next day delivery for Prime members, and at good legal bookshops such as Hammicks and Wildy & Sons.

We are regularly launching new books in our series of practical day-to-day practitioners' guides. Visit our website and join our free newsletter to be kept informed.

Lightning Source UK Ltd.
Milton Keynes UK
UKOW06f1122240617

303991UK00001B/10/P